BEGINNING

Bust of Master Cheng Man-ch'ing

T'AI CHI
STUDENTS' CONFESSIONS

the view from the back of the class

Paul H. Crompton Ltd
94 Felsham Road
London SW15 1DQ

*I would like to dedicate this book to Nigel Sutton whom I count
as my first real teacher and who lit the Tai Chi fire within me.*

*From there Master Tan Ching Ngee of Singapore and Masters
Liang He Ching, Tan Seow Theng, Koh Ah Tee of Malaysia fanned
that flame. Training with Peter Ralston and Willie Lim has continued
to prove to me that this is an ever evolving art and the fire is roaring.*

Mark Peters

Cartoons by Hunt Emerson: Largecow website

ISBN: 978-1-874250-86-9

Contents

Cartoons: Hunt Emerson

Mark Peters came to my attention through my eldest son, Matthew, who was living near him in Edgbaston, some years ago. Matthew trained with Mark and told me about him. Mark is a devoted student and teacher of the Tai Chi Chuan promoted by Master Cheng Man-ch'ing. Master Cheng was a pupil of Yang Cheng-fu, on whose methods most of the western world's Yang style training is based.

Master Cheng has received a mountain of praise and a few mole hills of criticism; the latter from people who never met him, which of course makes them eminently qualified ... The reasons for the criticism are not clear to me, and it is fruitless to guess what they may be based on. What is much clearer is that some people following in his footsteps have misunderstood his message. In the chapter of this book devoted to a visit from one of Master Cheng's pupils and a teacher in his own right, Master Tan, it is clear that Master Cheng did not limit himself to the ultra-soft looking movements, the ultra-slow movements to be seen on very old film, but explored a diversity of methods and speeds. Sadly, some of his pupils seem to have overlooked that fact and limited their training to very slow, very yielding action which in turn limits them. They can be described as getting only a part of the message. Therefore, such students cannot really describe themselves as Cheng Man-ch'ing practitioners in the full meaning of the word.

By reading this book you will get a taste of people training and studying tai chi with a large degree of open mind. Tai chi holds up a mirror to certain important aspects of life, of nature and of science. It recognises the ebb and flow inherent in everything, and says that to try to harden oneself, to resist and never to allow something to take place as distinct from making it take place is to be out of harmony with life itself.

This message appears time and again in this anthology from pupils and teachers. I believe it will be welcomed by everyone interested in this kind of subject.

Paul Crompton

Mark Peters leading a class in Form practise

Introduction

The chapters contained within this book were written by students and instructors, past and present, of the Kai Ming Association for Tai Chi Chuan, plus a few Tai Chi friends. Their occupations and ages are diverse to say the least, but all have one thing in common – their love and enthusiasm for Tai Chi Chuan.

It was written to allow beginners and would be students a glimpse into the benefits and sometimes tribulations they will experience along the path of this wonderful art.

Some improve physically, some mentally, but there is always a price to pay before we find ourselves in the place we want to be. Tai Chi is no exception; there are times that you will feel frustrated and times that you will feel elated. In the beginning you may feel it is much easier to give up than struggle on, wondering how anybody can understand its intricacies.

We hope you will be heartened by the stories written herein; they have been penned by ordinary people like you and me, who like you took the trouble to pick up a book with the hope that the knowledge within would lead them on a path which would enhance their lives.

We have all at sometime hidden 'at the back of the class' be it at school in our younger days or more recently at night school or a workshop etc. This anonymity gave us the chance to look at those around us as well as hide from the eye of those in charge. Come forward, read this book and make real the wondrous art of Tai Chi Chuan. Some chapters are light hearted, some in-depth but all are written in plain English with a view to demystify.

Mark Peters showing correct foot positions

Tai Chi from the Ground Up ...

Your "root" is already there for you. You don't have to "learn" how to get it – just stop fighting gravity!

Attributed to Cheng Man Ching

Professor Cheng is said to have told students to work with the idea of gravity and consider how it acts upon you. It is our job to achieve the alignment through the body that creates the correct structure to distribute the load most effectively. Some say we should 'claw' at the ground to gain connection and even 'paint it up' by stating that we are activating the 'bubbling well' by pulling up this point. The fact is although you may increase the awareness of this point by pulling it in, by the tension you have created, you will most certainly sever the natural connect that exists; Lao Tzu said nature is simple; we make it complicated and this is a prime example …

Everything in Tai Chi Chuan from standing post to combat is designed to harness your connection with the ground; we have evolved within a specific gravitational field that acts upon everything we do and are. By aligning ourselves effectively with it we can access and harness intrinsic power. Hey, remember the Superman films where he was incredibly strong because his home world's gravitational field was far more powerful than that of earth. Unfortunately I can't fly nor do I have x-ray eyes. Fantasy aside, physical proof of the effects of gravity can be found in astronauts where loss of bone density has been recorded following time spent in gravity free space; in addition to this, muscles and tissues waste away as they are not in use to the degree designed.

The basis of this article is to discuss the concept of structural alignment and the effects of gravity. I will introduce some of the games we play in our club and look at problems with kicks for instance. The aim is not to lay down definitive rules but to open discussions and consider a few concepts.

Many schools have their own Standing Post (Zhang Zhong) postures but for ease we will discuss the simplest, which most will known as Wu Chi. This involves standing in a relaxed posture with feet shoulder width and arms relaxed by your sides. Try and feel a line through your body from the Pai-Hui point (crown of your head) through your Dan Tien and into the Yong-Quan point in your feet. Let the body hang as if suspended from the Pai-Hui point and try to feel as if everything is stacked underneath like building blocks. The building blocks have to be in just the right place to allow gravity to act upon them and for them not to be unstable. Now stand for a few minutes with your eyes closed, joints soft, not locked and weight evenly distributed. Feel the ground with the *whole* contact area of your feet. Feel the effect of gravity acting upon you; do not resist by stiffening up and bracing your body, just relax and let the structure do the rest. Search your body with your mind's eye looking for slight mis-alignments and imbalances, and gently adjust. This alignment exercise helps to develop whole body awareness and build the compressive resilient energy called Pung (ward-off). Pung is the first, and most important, of the eight methods trained in Tai Chi Chuan. Discussions of the eight methods and five steps are beyond the scope of this article, and are readily available in many books including *Tai Chi Touchstones* by Douglas Wile. Remember 'structural alignment allows relaxation to occur'. Putting the body into imbalance (or mis-alignment) causes the muscles to devote some of their energy to trying to regain and maintain balance. The ensuing tension affects not only the body but also the mind causing distractions and extraneous thought processes.

Practicing slowly allows you to pay attention to every little detail to every aspect of every movement; it allows you to 'live in the moment' and pay attention to that moment rather than already thinking about and rushing to the next. I always break movement from one posture to the next into three simple stages: 1) step and ensure the ground is good beneath your foot 2) transfer your weight and align with gravity to ensure your balance is correct 3) turn about your new axis. Rushing this process is a common occurrence and people wonder why they are not balanced or their knee hurts or the waist movement has no power. Try it! Move how you normally would, then do it again and pay attention to the three stages; if you think you did it correctly, great, but when you turned did your knee move sideways? Did you feel your weight move in your foot? When you are about to turn, your hip/waist joint should already be lined up with your knee and foot. If it is, great again, I'll come to your class. Remember this article is called 'from the ground up', what I am attempting to do is build a structural awareness from the ground up.

There are a number of theories developed which go beyond the basic method we are all taught which is 'connect to the earth through the Yong-Quan point'. These include William Chen's 'Three Nail method' and Peter Ralston's 'Press the knee into the heel'. What they all appear to do is try to get the practitioner to allow the body weight to naturally fall to the ground and align everything correctly to create a natural resilient support. Focussing on specific points is as much a danger as it is a benefit if you do not understand what you are aiming for and what the underlying principle is; an example of this is if you focus on connecting the Yong-Quan point to the ground too much, you could empty the heel and toes thereby de-stabilising the longitudinal and transverse arches. This in turn could de-stabilise the knee and create excessive muscle tension as well as joint wear. Cheng Man Ch'ing's comments cannot be overlooked here; when asked by a student "When will my legs stop aching?", he replied "When you stop improving". Correct alignment allows the muscles to release any unnecessary tension and this release releases weight, previously held up, to fall naturally to the supports below, the most apparent of which are the major leg muscles.

Our initial response to loading a leg is to tighten the muscles to 'ready them' for the task at hand. This tightening is wasteful of energy and unnecessary, as everything exists within the body to perform the function automatically and in a relaxed manner. Research has shown that the function of the arch is as a shock absorber, essential not just while moving but also while stationary to take the first stage of loading. The spring ligament (plantar calcaneonavicular), as its name implies, offers a springy support and is the main element for the structure of the arch under normal load conditions. Research by Basmajian and Stecko (1963), and Gomez-Pellico and Llanos-Alcazar (1976) showed that ligaments give the initial support and muscles such as the Peroneus Longus gave additional support only as the load increased. As boring as this might sound, what it proves is muscle activity (let alone tension) is hardly required to support your mass so why waste the effort. We stand on our legs most of the time and pay little attention to what's going on, but as soon as an external load is applied by somebody pushing against us, doing squats with weights and so on, we start to resist and unnecessarily over-activate our muscles. The function of our mind is what makes the difference. Try to imagine *receiving* the additional load rather than resisting or pushing back against it and notice the difference in muscle activity; work with a partner to gain greater feedback. Remember *receive* doesn't mean *run away from*, it means to accept and make it part of you, or 'blend with' as they say in Aikido.

The next area of the body to look at is the pelvis. The muscles in and around this area are large and difficult to relax. One of my students is an osteopath and told me that more than 50% of his business involves working on problems due to tensions in the pelvic region. Most people are unaware of the amount of tension they hold; when we practice the loosening taught within our club you can see the gradual freeing and relaxation in this area more than any other; the exercises were originally developed by Huang Shyan Shen, a leading disciple of Cheng. Remember the Tai Chi classic, "The waist is the commander".

The best analogies I have come up with to describe this area are 'like a free running ball-bearing race' and 'like a ship's compass, free and self-levelling in all directions'. When you first feel it release, it is astounding; suddenly the whole body has a new feeling of freedom. The release allows a new level of sinking (or grounding) which increases your feeling of connection to the ground. A friend of mine has been practicing martial arts for twenty years and believed he was relaxed and fluid, that his training in Wing Chun and Filipino arts had taught him to flow with ease and power. But when he started push-hands with us he said he felt like wood. He tired quickly and had trouble getting a reference to strike from while I was inside his guard before he had chance to respond. It wasn't because I was better, only that his speed was from upper body power and the flow stopped at his waist. Once he started practicing the waist loosening exercises he had newly found power and speed unfortunately for me, but luckily he has still to discover his root. It is useful to know that the word 'waist' in English does not have the same meaning as that used in Chinese, in respect of Tai Chi. A clearer translation would be hip/waist which refers to the leg to pelvis joint known as the Qua or inguinal crease. Ankles, hips, wrists and shoulders are ball and socket whereas knees and elbows are hinge joints. If you think about this, to gain the freest movement in all directions joints should be kept roughly at midpoint. As tension is released and the body relaxes you will find that your joints will naturally rest near to their midpoint and correctly align with each other. From here, let the muscles/tissues of the midsection relax and drop to free all areas in and around the pelvic region. Now move to the upper body.

When students first come to our classes, we say 'Relax the shoulders', so much that the usual comment is they feel their shoulders are in their ears. Most of us have always been told, as far back as school, to 'Stand tall, shoulders back and chest out'. Unfortunately this causes tension, restricts movement and effects natural function. The classics say, "Sink the chest and pluck/lift the back", which, when taken literally, can cause hunching, not necessarily as bad as Quasimodo but still bad posture. By releasing the body and allowing it to naturally hang down, there is a natural sinking of the chest that in turn causes a natural filling or plucking of the back. Remember 'natural' not forced. The classics say we should be 'As if suspended from above' but I feel this would be clearer if it read 'as if suspended from above on a piece of suitable strength elastic'. I shouldn't think they had bungee jumping back then, or even those toy spiders that hang on elastic, so it needs a little expanding to allow analogies from our time to give a clearer reference. Try this out. Imagine your body is hanging from a piece of suitable strength elastic attached to the crown of your head, then imagine you are suspended by a piece of cord instead – can you feel the buoyancy needed for free movement with the elastic or does it feel a little dead or stilted with the cord? Sinking the chest allows the breath to fall and the sensation of 'hanging down' to improve.

What I mean by allowing the breath to fall is that there is a sensation of sinking inside the body whereby the breath appears to be pulled in and down by your stomach rather than feeling all chesty or pulled in by the expansion of your chest. What is actually happening is that you are using your diaphragm and therefore activating more of your lung capacity. Most of us usually breathe with our chest and only use the top third of our lungs; this is only really apparent to those suffering from asthma or anxiety attacks, which cause a feeling of tightness of the chest. Once mastered, abdominal breathing allows deeper natural breathing, which in turn improves oxygenation to the blood, which in turn increases oxygen to the organs, which in turn improves their function and so on.

I was always taught drop the shoulders, raise the hands and imagine there was a weight hanging from the elbows. The visualisation of the weight helps to drop the shoulders, but can also cause tension if the joints are not positioned properly. The outline of this is stated in the 'Yang Family 12 character motto' "Extend the elbows outward; leave a hollow in the armpits. The elbows pull down the tops of the shoulders, connect the wrists and carry along the fingers." (Yang Zhenduo, Yang Shih Taiji, 1997). The positioning of the elbow opens the shoulder and allows the joint to fall into place; from here the hand can sit virtually on top of the wrist as favoured by Cheng Man Ching. I really like an idea developed by Peter Ralston which he calls 'hand up – you down' whereby as you raise your hand you have the sensation that everything else is falling/sinking down; awareness of your body is needed to allow you to feel and release or 'drain away' any tensions. Maybe this is the feeling Cheng had when he dreamed that his arms were broken, then when he woke nobody could defeat him. These ideas are designed to release any predisposition to use muscular force of the arm, rather than alignment with the ground, to apply power through compression. In fact, in application, you do not hit your target, you simply put yourself in the way and let the alignment between the target and the ground do the work. This is sometimes a hard concept to grasp as why would anybody walk on to a strike, but if you consider in attacking, they have to come towards you, simplistically all you have to do is put yourself in the right place and be correctly aligned; the difference is in the thought process between an attack and a gift – all attacks are gifts because the attacker is committing himself – but this is another article in itself.

The above areas need to be worked with and developed in a stationary position before we work with the principles of movement described next.

There are lots of discussions, be they poetic, on the use of bows in the body or 'seek the straight within the curve' or rotate 'like a wheel' but how do they apply to body movement for health and martial application? You have all most likely heard that Tai Chi movements are circular rather than linear, but why, when others tell us that the shortest distance between two points is a straight line? We could expand the statement to say 'the straightest line of least resistance' which could be another way of saying 'seek the straight within the curve'. We have all heard the saying 'stuck in a rut' or seen the evidence that going backwards and forwards over the same spot wears it out quickly, but have you ever considered linear movement of the joints can have the same effect? It can wear away the cartilage cushion separating the joints, which eventually leads to osteoarthritis. Once formed, ruts are very difficult to get out of, plus they limit the mobility and life of the joints. Tai Chi's smooth rounded movements work joints through their full range thereby aiding mobility and removing the risk of grooves forming. In addition to this, linear movements allow direct force to be applied, risking impact shock back to you as well as giving your opponent a point of reference. Imagine catching a cricket ball, it has a direction and velocity which, if you position yourself in its path to catch it, it will hurt. An experienced catcher will follow the trajectory and either slow the ball for a catch or redirect it back, through a curved path, to another player. This is the redirection of force as applied in Tai Chi Chuan. By keeping the joints soft (not locked) curves are naturally formed which can be springy (pung) and act as the body's natural shock absorbers.

Now your body is soft and springy, you have allowed gravity to act on you and align with it, your joints are loose and free. Everything is wonderful, but what happens when you lift one leg off the floor? Can you still apply the same principles? *Do* you still apply the same principles? The answer should be an emphatic '*yes*'! To repeat a statement I made earlier. "Practicing slowly allows you to pay attention to every little detail of every aspect of every movement", in addition to this it now allows you to pay attention to what is happening throughout your body and how you relate to the gravitational pull acting on you. I also mentioned three stages to movement, the third stage now is not just to turn the waist but also to lift the leg to its new position. Nigel Sutton always told me "When applying kicks, always keep three legs on the ground", by which he meant one of your legs and the two of your opponent; this is to ensure a stable foundation, but what do you do when there is nobody to hang on to? The same principles apply whether you are raising your leg to move to a new position or a single leg posture: know your centre and move from it, keep your hips level and balanced, do not raise your hip/body when you raise the limb, ensure body unity, and so on. By seeking stillness in movement, as we are told, the true essence of 'Tai Chi for self-defence' comes into play. We are able to defend against the wear-and-tear of our daily life, improving our well-being for now and the future.

We have built the body from the ground up like a series of blocks, not rigid blocks, but blocks that are allowed to naturally compress under the load of those above and achieve natural alignment. The elastic cord is a means of supporting or suspending (to allow you to hang down) to prevent misalignment. As stated, we do not have to create this rooted alignment; it is already there if we could but see. Once you can *give up* to the idea, 'invest in loss' as Cheng was fond of saying, your development in the art of Tai Chi Chuan goes beyond the superficial 'feel good' shapes and is allowed to become a *real* method of martial and health development. Isador Rabi (Nobel prize winner in physics) said, "Life is too short to spend your time doing something because someone else said it was important. You must feel the thing yourself ..." Enjoy the experimentation and do not accept everything at face value. Do not just go through the motions because all around you are, because the shapes and methods are familiar and safe, strive for the essence of the art and to the true understanding of the nature of things.

Garry Clarke and Mark Peters

3

Tai Chi and Health

Keeping healthy is one of the main aims of those who practice Tai Chi. Hence it is most appropriate to pose the question: how does Tai Chi contribute to my health and wellbeing?

In the warm up exercises (Chi Kung), the rhythmic movements help the muscles and joints and keep the circulation active. The breathing exercises are vital for the lungs. The regular deep breathing energises the systems and increases the oxygen intake of the body. At all times breathing should be through the nose not the mouth. Breathing should be coordinated with the body movement. The general rule is that you inhale when you contract or pull back, exhale when you expand or strike.

The regular exercises help create the feeling of well being. It is a known fact that exercises produce endorphins. Production of endorphins in the brain induces the sense of well-being and happiness. Of course some people are happier than others during the classes; this depends on the level of endorphins, besides other factors. Doing the exercises in the open air is another benefit. Fresh air contains more oxygen, and is more energising to the individual. Practising the form at home is better if you have more space to move. If these practices are carried out in an open space as in the garden, the benefit will be greater. However, avoid slippery surfaces.

Tai Chi helps you to be more aware of your surroundings. The more you practice, the more aware you are of the environment around you. To increase this awareness, you can practice parts of the form with eyes closed. One needs to be careful when changing orientation such as in turning and kicking with the sole and sweeping in the lotus movements (when you turn 180°). If you practice Tai Chi on this deeper level, your process of "anticipation" will increase through your increased awareness of your surroundings.

Posture is emphasised in all Tai Chi sessions, especially in "the form". Maintaining a straight back cannot be stressed enough. The spine should be held straight and vertical. One of the scourges of our present day life is backache. Training oneself to straighten the back is a great asset in life, more so as one advances in age. Tai Chi practitioners should use the chance of practising the art to acquire the habit of having a straight back. The more self conscious you are about that most important posture, the more it becomes a habit.

Tai Chi has a calming effect on the individual, and in our present day stresses and tribulations that is an asset. Here, concentration and proper regular breathing during the sessions is of help. To get the full benefit of the sessions, a calm mind and a relaxed body are beneficial. In turn, the practice of Tai Chi will increase the calmness and relaxation. People will notice that as they practice Tai Chi, and for that matter any other self defence art, they will be more aware of what they eat and drink. One hopes that those practising the art will realise the futility of the habit of smoking. Those who attend the summer-long weekend training held in Unstone Grange will notice the healthy food provided.

Muscles and bones benefit from the exercises and form. The muscle tones well, rather than enlarges, owing to the gentle nature of the form. The bones are rendered firmer and healthier. As a matter of fact, Tai Chi is beneficial for sufferers of osteoporosis, though the exercises in these cases should be carefully monitored by the trainers. Related to the above point is the help Tai Chi lends to balance.

Master Cheng Man-Ch'ing, who simplified Tai Chi to its present form, was a doctor and professor of Chinese Medicine. He directed many of his patients to take up Tai Chi. He believed that such practice would help his patients in combating their illnesses and enhance their recovery. The basis of Chinese Medicine is the Yin and Yang, the same has great significance for Tai Chi. There has been much research in Tai Chi and Health and the benefits have been proven through vigorous scientific methodology.

References:
1. *Teach yourself Tai Chi*. Robert Parry. Teach Yourself Books, Hodder and Stoughton, London, 2001.
2. *Tai Chi – The Supreme Ultimate*. Lawrence Galante. Samuel Weiser, York Beach, Maine, 1981.

Tai Chi in the park, Cannon Hill Park, Birmingham

Jenny Peters with Tai Chi Fan

4

Seeking the Way

During my Tai Chi journey I have met many teachers and practitioners who have seemed to me "harmony with this earth" personified, and at peace with themselves. I have also met many, like myself, who would like to attain this state, and who spend many hours examining how they can achieve it, this Nirvana.

However as I struggled to have "kind feelings" for some of my fellow beings, I believed that it was probably way, way beyond my capabilities. In fact upon enquiring of these "peaceful warriors" what their way to enlightenment had been, many of them wondered what I meant. They just *were*!

Now unless there is a superhuman gene out there, I feel that they must have had help from somewhere to guide them to the "right path".

Cheng Man Ch'ing, the founder of our style of Tai Chi, followed the teachings of Confucius, but as with many things in life, until recently that fact had just been there. We had never as a club fully understood how much of an influence it may have had on him, and our form. Also we had never thought about the fact that maybe we as individuals might benefit by looking into the teachings of this revered man.

Tai Chi is considered a Taoist art, but what does this really mean? Our Association is lucky enough to have a great scholar and philosopher as one of our students and trainee instructors. This man spent his whole life, and I quote, "Cultivating the mind but neglecting his physical body", and so eventually his body complained. He developed high blood pressure. Maybe this was due to lack of exercise, stress of preparing and delivering lectures around the world, where good food and good wine could be par for the course. This may sound quite a nice existence, but eventually the piper has to be paid!

As a nurse I see this all the time. Whatever job we have and however much we enjoy it some people are always in fifth gear. When I ask my patients, "Do you get any regular exercise?",which I see as "time out" for themselves, they invariably reply, "Oh yes, I'm always running round at work, in the office, factory, building site, supermarket," and so forth. They are quite surprised when I tell them this is *not* the exercise I mean. What they perceive as "good" for them is in fact not.

They are generally racing round to meet time schedules, get more done, finish something that is urgent before they leave work, catch up with something they had forgotten to do earlier.

This is not good for you. It is adrenaline induced "exercise" which can be the worst kind.

Heart racing, mind racing, stress, stress, stress. I like this definition of Stress: *doing more but achieving less*. I look on regular exercise as going to a gym, swimming, sports or yes, Tai Chi.

But I digress. This professor came to our club to try and find healing for his neglected body, but he was such a learned man and so interesting to chat to we then thought maybe others in the Association would like to learn more about Taoism, and we where lucky enough to have the ideal teacher right here with us. Although he is quite a humble man and was sceptical as to what format he could present for a workshop/discussion on this subject he finally agreed to go away and research further into this vast area. He came back to Mark Peters with the outline for three seminars.

These were:

    I.   Taoism
    II.   Confucianism.
    III.   Buddhism.

In that order.

Included in each was a meditation session that related to that workshop. We have now run these twice within our club. What began as a simple idea turned out to be a wonderful learning experience, which was so much more than any of us expected. It has allowed many of us to believe that maybe we can, or already are, leading a way of life we believed we would never attain. It has brought so much into our lives and I think a greater understanding of just "being".

Before completing these seminars I had listened to a recording of an interview with the Dalai Lama who said that one of the teachings of

Buddhism was to accept that we are put on this earth to be happy and should strive to attain this. At the time I did not understand the relevance of this statement and thought surely this is a selfish introverted attitude.

During the Buddhism seminar discussions within our club the reason for this was explained. Happy people spread happiness. Being unhappy may be the selfish element within us, for we can be so focused on our own unhappy state they we drag others down with us! Think about it. By the end of our workshops I felt that Taoism led into Confucianism and Confucianism blended into Buddhism. Threads can link them all. You need to put yourself right, Taoism, before you can help the whole, Confucianism and then spread the happiness, Buddhism. This of course is my own simplified understanding of what I believe to be the essence of living a more contented life.

Obviously not everyone wants to delve further than a weekly Tai Chi class, but for all of us within Kai-Ming who took part in these days there was a huge consensus of their great value as a club and as individuals.

Thank you David.

"IF I CAN HAVE SOMEONE ELSE I'LL SHOW YOU THAT AGAIN!"

Confessions of a Pusher

A few weeks ago, I had a revelation. One of those moments of absolute clarity when something that you previously did not understand, suddenly becomes perfectly obvious.

My moment of insight came shortly after the Spring Camp at Unstone Grange, and was caused by events at that camp. I had been pushing hands with a student who attends the class at which I assist. During the session, he managed to push me off-balance twice. How did I feel? Well, actually, I was pleased to see the increase in skill demonstrated by "my" student. I also felt that I was taking the occasional "defeat" well, ... investing in loss. Lao Tsu wrote "Gentle the will in order to strengthen the bones", and Cheng Man Ching taught that before one can aspire to the highest levels of Tai Chi Chuan abilities, the ego must be suppressed. He exhorts us to become mild and gentle in demeanour, rather than arrogant and over-inflated, and to invest in loss. Surely I was doing just that.

After a while, we changed partners, and I found myself standing opposite one of the most senior of our instructors. After ten minutes of earnest effort, I hadn't once come near to disturbing this man's equilibrium. He, on the other hand, with the softest of hands, had tipped, toppled, pulled, pushed and turned me to every point of the compass. How did I feel? Well, actually, ... bloody frustrated! I berated myself for lack of sensitivity and little or no rooting ability, and resolved to get in a lot more Push Hands practice.

It was only some days later, when mulling over these events, that I suddenly thought, "Why was I not equally as pleased to invest in loss at the

hands of one of my teachers, as I was at the hands of one of my students?"
And then the blinding light hit me, like Saul on the road to Damascus. I
hadn't suppressed the old enemy – ego – after all. It was still there, as
arrogant as ever. I took pleasure in being pushed off-balance by my student
because it proved what a great teacher I am, imparting skills effortlessly. I
didn't react quite so well to being pushed by my teacher, because my ego
couldn't find a good enough excuse.

Thanks to this insight, I'm on my guard again. I have renewed my battle
to suppress the ego. I will treat every occasion that I am pushed off-balance
as a tiny step in the learning process, no matter who does the pushing. I
resolve to become a better person. Now where's that newest student? I
want to show him how easily I can uproot him.

*(To "invest in loss" was a phrase used by Master Cheng to denote not
meeting force with force, but to yield even to the extent of allowing
oneself to be pushed off balance, for the sake of learning and
experiencing the process, thereby becoming able to accommodate the
push without losing balance – Publisher's note)*

Unstone Grange – 18 to 20 June 1999

The opportunity to spend a weekend at a Derbyshire Retreat with the promises of no cooking, cleaning or washing up, no telephone and television was not be missed. So it was on a glorious Friday evening we started out – the journey was about 2 hours; not too far, but far enough to make it a welcome escape from day to day routine. Sadly, the house itself is a little neglected, however the peace and tranquillity of the grounds more than made up for it.

Pre-supper activities consisted of a session in the Indian Sweat Tents for some, for others a meander around the kitchen garden, guessing what might be on the menu, was delightful. After a beautiful warm evening on Friday, Saturday dawned cold and cloudy – well it was the weekend after all! Nevertheless, Chi Gung before breakfast was well attended. The experience of practising Tai Chi outside in the fresh air is particularly special and really does set you up for the day – if only I could make the effort to do this every morning! After breakfast we all re-convened on the lawn around the garden pond to practice Yang Cheng Fu's Ten Essential Points of Tai Chi Chuan.

For me this was a most enlightening morning. Whilst I had heard these points explained and discussed many times, it was probably this particular morning that I actually started to understand a little more of their meaning and relevance. Not just their relevance to Tai Chi practice, but how this over-runs into day to day living. Let me try to explain what I mean:

"Suspended head – the head should be upright so that the spirit can reach the top." It was quite extraordinary how much the form fell apart if practiced with a "floppy" head. This leads to the question of how much can your day to day life fall apart if you walk around with "floppy" head looking at the ground? Just see how much more confident and positive you can be simply by walking around with your head held upright.

"Differentiate between full and empty".

This is probably the first point we learn as new practitioners of Tai Chi – how much time have we spent walking forwards and backwards, up and down halls? The yin and yang – balance and compromise – that's what life is all about and what makes the world go round!

"Use the mind, not force."

We practiced resisting force with physical strength and then by concentrating the mind on resisting the same force – the results were quite dramatic! For me, this simply demonstrated the power of positive thinking. Set your goals in life, short term or big picture, and believe you can achieve them – you will!

After lunch the sessions continued outside with time spent practising warm up exercises and "five animals" The afternoon concluded with weapons training and form play with some of us managing to learn a complete new form!

Sunday afternoon saw a continuation of the weapons training of Saturday. However many were simply happy to sit and chat quietly in the sunshine or take advantage of the services of our own reflexologist, who was on hand, or on foot even, for those who wanted to experience this remarkable complementary therapy.

The whole weekend was relaxing, refreshing and invaluable. The benefits of spending uninterrupted time practising Tai Chi are absolute. Unfortunately for most of us, the day to day commitments of work, home and family usually don't allow this amount of time to be spent in training. However, having recognised the advantages that consistent training can offer, perhaps we should be aiming for more weekends away?

Training in Tai Chi Chi Kung (Qigong)

"Stay sung (relax). When practicing the form you must keep relaxed. In time you will find that it will become part of your physical and mental state."

Cheng Man Ching (1947)

7

Tai Chi by Osmosis

Many people give up before they gain any real benefits or fail to realise why they make no progress. Tai Chi by its very nature involves a great deal of patience due to the detail and level of personal development required. Where failure occurs is the false idea that as it is a gentle art, little or no effort is required for progress. Skills cannot be developed without effort and a practical understanding of what you are doing. This is no different whether training in the East or West other than that in the East a larger percentage of the population practice daily, and due to cultural make-up, the majority believe that by daily practice alone they will achieve the benefits they strive for. Western society is less patient and more demanding; in general we want it to work now and to quote in instructor from Stourport, expect that "floating around the room listening to flute music" is all that is needed. Professor Cheng is quoted as saying that Tai Chi without practical application gives superficial benefits at best, but maybe superficial benefits are all you require …

Tai Chi skill, or skill in any art for that matter, cannot be obtained by osmosis – by being in close proximity to a skilled practitioner and absorbing their ability by association. Constant searching is required and I don't mean for a teacher who can offer supposed sort cuts; search within yourself to gain a clear understanding of your goals; search for information beyond that of your teacher alone to gain clarification and cross-reference. There are no secrets in Tai Chi. Everything is obtainable by all of us with patience and perseverance. Practitioners in the East who have become Masters in their own right have done so by breaking the mould and realising they cannot 'catch' Tai Chi ability but have to work at it with an inquisitive mind, always searching, testing and re-checking what they are doing against the accepted standards laid down in the classics. In the West we are supposed to have more inquisitive minds but in the main seem to switch this mind off when studying Tai Chi. As an engineer I tend to look at what I do in a mechanical way: structural alignment, kinetic and potential energy, mechanical function of the organs and so on. This has given me a reference point from my daily life and therefore a constant check of practical appreciation. Although it has helped, it is not a prerequisite that you are an engineer or medically trained to gain an appreciation of Tai Chi. Yang Cheng Fu was virtually illiterate and nobody doubts his abilities ...

There are many tools for development within the art and apart from the 'standards' that will be discussed below, each school or style usually has something of its own. For example the silk reeling exercises of Chen style. I practice Cheng style (sometimes referred to as Yang short form) as developed by Professor Cheng Man Ch'ing of Taiwan. In addition to the standards, we practice five animal exercises developed by Professor Cheng and five loosening exercises developed by Huang Shyan Shen; Huang was one of Cheng Man Ch'ing's most senior students and disciples teaching mostly in Malaysia and Singapore. Both of these sets develop looseness (Fang Song) and detailed body connection/co-ordination that is at the essence of this style. In Mark Henssesy's book 'Master of Five Excellences' there is a translated work by Cheng Man Ch'ing on the method and value of the 'constant bear' exercise.

All styles have methods of developing ward-off energy (Pung) which is the first of the eight core methods. This can be described as a springy resilient energy similar to that felt if you squeeze a tennis ball or the buoyancy of an object that floats on water. Many practice standing post (Zhang Zhong) as a standard method of training this energy; although this can develop a very powerful ward-off, the bear exercise develops a more lively word-off which allows you to receive energy/force and still maintain your structure. There are many picture and video footage of Professor Cheng and other Tai Chi Masters warding-off the push of a line of strong people; this is really a trick to wow the crowds as is the unbendable arm of Aikido and board breaking of Karate and Taekwondo, a bi-product of a core skill. A lively ward-off would never allow any force to land on it, as the classics say, "A feather may not be added or a fly alight". This is not magic trick nor an esoteric use of Chi but a method of correct and dedicate training, something we can all achieve. I remember seeing Keith Chegwin, on the Channel 4 Big Breakfast show, talking to a supposed Tai Chi practitioner. As the guy stood in a typical lift-hands posture from his form, Keith talked to him about calm balance and tranquillity that is typified by Tai Chi and the guy agreed; Keith pushed him slightly and the guy fell over. I know it was embarrassing for him, on TV, but how can he say 'It's Tai Chi' if he couldn't even stand up properly …

The *standards* most schools/styles practice are empty-hand form, push-hands (Tui Shou), breathing exercises (Qigong), Standing post (Zhang Zhong) and weapons. Empty-hand form teaches controlled body co-ordination, balance, basic martial application and self-awareness. Push-hands teaches balance, space awareness, sensitivity and how to deal with giving and receiving force/energy. Qigong teaches mind and body connection through breath awareness. Standing post teaches the structural alignment and mental condition required to balance the ward-off energy between the effects of gravity and the ground underneath your feet. Weapons each has its own flavour and teach core principles and attributes required for proper application. For example the straight sword (Jen) teaches sensitivity, quick loose reflexes and agile footwork. The Broadsword or Sabre (Dao) teaches coiling and builds strong waist movement excellent for wrestling and locks as well as strengthening the kidneys and digestive system.

Tai Chi Chuan professes to be an art of scholars and spiritually developed people rather than the brutish hacking of the more overtly physical systems. Unfortunately this has led to a myriad of self-proclaimed Masters who appear to 'talk a good fight' and make constant references to classical texts but do not apply the principles stated as they have no real understanding of practical application. The great Chinese ruler Wang An Shi [Yang Fang period circa 1078-1085] thought little of the professors of his day, calling them "men of merely literary ability". As a student he refused to sit his final exams, and when in power, he personally supervised the contents of exam papers to ensure the content was practical and relevant. Don't get me wrong, books have their place and are essential reference tools, with contemporary classics such as "There Are No Secrets" by Wolf Lowenthal being an inspiration to us all. Reading is an enjoyable pastime and we do absorb knowledge. I quote in class from books I have read as well as directly from my teachers, all the time. What I am saying is you can't quote stuff if you don't practice it or at least strive to understand it. You can't just *be* single-weighted because your teacher says you should, you have to understand what is meant by it and strive to attain it with the assistance of your instructor and classmates. I entitled the article 'Tai Chi by Osmosis' because to a small degree we do absorb directly from our teacher and classmates, but unfortunately this is not always a good thing. My wife told me years ago that I had subconsciously started an 'affected cough' the same as my teacher at the time. Those of us who learned to drive or have taught a friend or partner may have noticed mannerisms carried across.

To progress in this wondrous art, like all things in life, it takes diligent practice. Find a good teacher but don't take everything at face value; decide what you want from your training and what is needed to achieve it. Achieve the spiritual through the physical; in this I mean develop a deeper understanding and development through practical training and application. This does not mean test your art by fighting others. Self-defence in Tai Chi is as much self-defence from an external attacker as in internal attacker; general wear and tear, stress, and so on. I joke in class about this but Tai Chi really is *buy one get one free*; you come for relaxation and get a system of self-defence, you come for self-defence and get a method of relaxation, there's no need to do Yoga and Kick-boxing. Train effectively, with a good heart and open mind and you can surpass the skills of your teachers, for Tai Chi knows no bounds. When you feel you have something to offer others drop me a line and I'll come and train with you …

The true art of relaxation …

8

Tai Chi and Weight Training

Tai Chi Chuan mainly works on strengthening the legs, because it is believed that you die from the feet upwards, so healthy legs means in theory it stops you from leaving this sphere prematurely. If you use Tai Chi as just a source of well being then this is fine, but to use it as martial art you need more of an all over body strength which can be demonstrated in some of the many forms of fast, fighting and weapon forms of Tai Chi Chuan.

In essence it is unreasonable that a person would be able to fend off an attack from nowhere, that is, unless you were Inspector Clueso. I'm not saying that Tai Chi would not be any help at all because it would give a relaxed body, structurally sound is heavier and harder to manipulate, but after this initial attack you could be in a position where you are grappling and so forth. This then would be likely to proceed to physical force from the defender to at least get into position where he/she can use Tai Chi Chuan. All of the masters I have had the pleasure of training with over my time practicing Tai Chi have had incredible strength both mentally and physically. This is not by accident; a lot of their time includes strength training, which is done in various ways depending on their backgrounds. One of the reasons I am writing this article is to introduce the possibility of using weight training to enhance your Tai Chi and inevitably your overall health.

I have been playing with Tai Chi Chuan now for about twelve years and dabbled with other training regimes to complement my training. The reason have done this is probably because I come from a background of doing Karate, Judo and Kung Fu training even though I started Tai Chi Chuan from a purely health aspect. Students coming into Tai Chi Chuan from the same sort of background can often be left feeling empty and unfulfilled from a normal Tai Chi class. This is because a lot of martial arts classes consist of push up, crunches, running and non-stop punching and kicking routines, so after the class the student knows he/she has done something because it hurts.

Tai Chi classes concentrate mainly on the relaxation side and it depends on your level of relaxation to what you get out of the fist initial ten to twenty classes. I was once told that you don't need any other training if you do the whole form properly; this is because the form has a self regulation system to make the body constantly push itself. Basically you have two variables: body strength and the amount the body can relax. The more the body can relax the more the muscles have to work so they get stronger. The stronger the body becomes the more you can relax, so you can see that it is a perpetual circle of progress and if this sort of training can be obtained then after doing your Tai Chi form you will know that you have done something. Unfortunately before a student attains this realisation they have ceased training and we as westerners lead easier lives and are not exercised by the chores of day-to-day life, as were our mentors.

So increasing the strength of your body can only be a good thing, also weight training and Tai Chi do have a few things in common. One of these is slow controlled movement, paying attention to the details of the form and using the breath to connect our thoughts to our movements. This is so the body can learn to be more efficient, stronger and use the mind to focus on the task at hand because the brain is also learning, becoming more comfortable with the movement, which again makes it stronger and more efficient. If you start any exercise for the first time it is always hard, but the next time or the time after that depending on time constraint, all of a sudden it becomes easier. This is not because you have become stronger but because your body and brain have learned the movements so making it seem easier. I wonder why we do forms or kata's over and over again, hmmm! And from this, once the body is comfortable with the movement the layers of detail can be stripped away allowing you to look deeper into the finer points like the attention to various principles governing your movements.

If you do start weight training as a part of your Tai Chi experience then there are a few things to note. Tai Chi does emphasise using the whole body as one unit, but lifting weights usually means using individual muscles in isolation. If you use your imagination to feel that a connection exists between the movement, breath and the rest of the body then this can make your postures stronger, I also do slow more resistive movements rather than jerking the weight as this can lead to injury and doesn't complement the sort of movement needed in Tai Chi. I do not do any lifting with my legs. I stick to mountain biking, because I've found that doing exercises like squats actually destroys your root. I believe this is because the legs are learning to push off instead of loading. Usually the legs in Tai Chi receive force and loads the leg muscles just like a spring and then uses this stored energy, but lifting does seem to deaden this process. Mountain biking or just cycling does have a few benefits like balance, sensing the contact between you the bike and the floor and loading the legs to get force transferred to the ground instead of lifting out of your saddle losing power especially on soft or slippery surfaces. Another thing to consider is that all muscles should be exercised equally. Muscles usually have an opposing muscle like the biceps and triceps. The triceps extends the forearm and the biceps pull it back in. These muscles do work in harmony, one watching over the other. If this harmony is upset by one muscle being stronger than the other when the weaker muscle needs to react quickly; the stronger muscle may hinder it, working against it, but this is lessened in Tai Chi if the person can relax enough, making the muscle work faster and stronger. For training purposes you can get maybe two people to push hands and stop at time intervals and get a third person to feel the muscles that react or don't react to certain postures. I recently found that if someone pushes me say with a double push, and you help the push by adding to his or her push as a sort of hug, their own muscles work against them stopping their initial push.

Also I have found that little amounts of force applied to the right spot totally negates some attacks leaving you with almost nothing to do, but to just stand there, which when looking back at some of the masters I have trained with or footage I have seen, is what I have been searching for, but didn't know it. I have been practicing Tai Chi now for thirteen years and in that time I have realised that nothing should be taken for granted, from the breath you take, the move you make, and the thought you think. It can either work against you or for you, it is just a case of introducing yourself to the meanderings of the rivers and stillness of the mountains.

WHITE CRANE SPREADS WINGS

9

The House that Studies Circles

A personal view

Hi, my name is Perry I attend the 8-9 class at Selly Oak on Wednesdays. I first got involved in the martial art in 1977 when I joined a club in Kings Norton Birmingham. There I studied judo, aikido, kendo, atemi-jutsu and karate. For those unsure what these are here is a very brief description.

Judo – the gentle way

A competitive sport where you throw, hold down, choke, strangle and lock the arms of an opponent to win a contest. This should be one third of your study randori and kata being the rest. Randori is free practice and katas are prearranged forms of demonstration. To achieve progress in judo we are guided by the cyclic principles of nature, which if we look, are all around us.

Aikido – harmony way

In aikido we are defending ourselves only we take, re-direct, control and throwaway the techniques involved, called projections and locks, are spectacular and destructive; you do not w ant to be on the receiving end of these techniques. I repeat in Aikido we are defending ourselves only we also make use of nature's cyclic principles; a bewitchingly beautiful art evolved as a way of disarming swordsmen.

Kendo – the way of the Sword

We equip ourselves with protective equipment (face mask, Padded gloves and bamboo breast-plate) and set about striking the protected areas of an opponent with our sword. The sword is made from pieces of bamboo and blunted so no injuries can occur. When a strike is mad e we emit a "kiai": a loud scream that focuses our minds and energies, we are at one with ourselves when we hit. Again we randori and we learn katas-it becomes what it is: a thing of beauty.

Karate

We turn our bodies into weapons. We punch; we kick; we block; we contest; we randori and we kata. If we study long enough we discover aikido, we become enlightened: we no longer block, we move, we parry and strike back.

Atemi – jutsu

While studying the above we put them all to use in Forms and we defend ourselves. When we atemi we are striking. We strike with karate based blows. We know where to strike. If the atemi is not enough we follow up with the appropriate technique with use of control and ki-ai. We have many techniques to choose from because we are Budoka. We have studied more than one art. We observe the principle of reaction and non-resistance; we yield but don't submit. We feel confident and healthy; we avoid confrontation, Never lose control and respect ourselves and others. We train for life and succeed in daily life. "A recurring ankle injury meant the end of my physical study of the Japanese arts; also my Sensei (teacher) died two Christmas's ago and so, in my mind, did that part of my life.

I had gone full circle- the cycles had stopped, or so I thought. I began to miss the arts, and felt I was not being true to myself by not doing them. In August 2000 I joined the Kai-Ming Association and began to learn something 'new', soon the joy and wonder returned.

I have noticed our Tai Chi is very similar in spirit and movement, indeed one (at this stage of learning) of the techniques is the same: e.g. Chin-Na is nikkio in aikido. There are circular actions involved and I am studying them again. Once again I am in a house that studies circles.

Enjoy your art and your practice.

10

Have I Met a True Tai Chi Master?

A strange thing happened to me a few weeks ago which I thought may be of interest readers. I was crouching in my living room with both feet on the ground, when my ten week old Labrador Collie X – a magnificent creature, bounded up to me and placed his foot on the point of my knee. Now, I weigh eleven and a half stone (about 160 lb.) and felt fairly stable. He weighs about 18 lb.. For some inexplicable reason I found myself falling backwards, almost in slow motion yet with not enough time to get my hand out to steady myself. It was almost as if I was totally disorientated. Having hit terra firma and regained my senses I immediately thought that my dog must be, just had to be, a Tai Chi master reincarnated. This however was immediately dispelled as he ran over and bit me on the nose – Tai Chi masters don't do that apparently – but nevertheless, how did a small puppy push me over, and why couldn't I stop him? It also brought to mind some ancient Tai Chi saying about using a force of 4 oz to move a bull.

Okay, so the dog pushed me over by accident and just caught me in the right place at the right time and with the right pressure – which tells us something about our nervous system. If the push had been harder then my sensory nervous system would have located it and body reflexes would have responded to try and keep my balance. I may or may not have hit the floor but would have done so in a set of jerky movements as over compensations set in, due to reflex muscle spasms trying to maintain some sort of body alignment.

At the end of the day we are a bag of neurological reflexes, and to have an output, or motor response, we need a sensory input. We interact constantly with our environment both consciously and unconsciously. If we are unable to sense the force coming in then there is not a lot we can do about it until it is too late. As soon as we lose our centre of gravity, we tend to disorientate, rather than correct. Our reaction to a hard shove or trip is usually to the sense of the force applied, not our sense of our centre of gravity moving outside our stable base. This is shown majestically in Tim Cartnell's videos on throwing (which everyone should buy), and we should all be encouraged in this art of minimal effort, maximum results – something that Mark drums into us, week in and week out. If my 10 week old dog can do it, surely so can we.

11

Tai Chi and Golf

I started playing Golf and practising Tai Chi more or less at the same time. I found it most interesting that the two complement each other. To start with, when it comes to the way one stands at the very start, feet kept shoulder width apart. That is common in both golf and Tai Chi. In golf there are variations depending on what club is used and what shot is contemplated. In Tai Chi, this shoulder apart distance is followed in many warm up exercises and in different parts of the form.

From the very start in both, one need to learn to concentrate and be focused. In golf this is best noticed in the top professionals when screened on TV, you can see how concentrated in their thoughts they are during their play. In Tai Chi it is most apparent when you actively practice Tai Chi, you lose concentration and the next thing is you lose your balance. Keeping the balance is vital in both.

Keeping the balance, in both, depends on several factors, namely the way one stands, the distribution of weight between both feet, being well grounded, keeping the back straight and proper care of the position of the hands. The distribution of weight between both feet is so vital in learning the form in Tai Chi that books explaining the form devote much attention to this point . In Tai Chi, the range for having the weight of one foot or the other on the ground is from 0-100%.

In golf, the range also can be from 0-100%. Thus in the start of the back swing, the weight is equally distributed between both feet, whereas at the end of the forward swing, 100% is on the left leg, the right has only the toes touching the ground. Between these two extremes, there is a wide variation depending on the shot played. In Tai Chi you learn that twisting round should be from the waist, with the hips opening and closing depending on the direction of the twist. In golf, both in the downswing and upswing, hands and shoulders should move in unison, this does entail by necessity that the movement should be from the waist, also opening and closing the hip joints.

To have a proper and balanced movement, the feet should be well grounded, in that both Tai Chi and golf agree. In golf, in the backswing, the weight on the feet should be 50/50 and the feet should be well grounded. In Tai Chi, if you are not well grounded you lose balance and fall. To help the grounding, in both, you bend the knees slightly. You also make note not to have the knees beyond the the balls of the feet. Also, in both, attention to the position of the chin is important, not too high nor too low. In golf a too low a chin will bring the face below the left shoulder at the end of the backswing preventing proper sighting of the ball.

In both, to help the proper balance, you need the back to be straight. Tai chi teaches how to be aware of your surroundings. Some exercises are carried out with the eyes closed. In golf it helps to be aware of your surroundings. This is amply illustrated when you lose a ball. If you are aware of your shot, you can have a rough idea where the ball landed and this awareness can help finding it. Awareness provides the feedback that enables you to have an idea of the direction and distance the ball travelled. Visualisation is helpful in both golf and Tai Chi.

In Tai Chi you learn how to control breathing. In golf you can control and adjust your breathing to fit in with your shots. It is apparent that there are many similarities between Tai Chi and golf. A golfer will benefit from practising Tai chi. Further, he/she would have some relaxing and useful exercises during winter when the golf courses can be unmanageable. A keen Tai Chi person will find that his experience will help him take up golf easier. Golf and Tai Chi are complementary.

12

My View from the Back of the Class

I heard of Tai Chi years ago when a friend of mine began to practice in London's Chinatown. But then I moved, and have only recently re-settled back in the U.K. During the long years away, karate or judo were the only martial arts on offer. All that chopping and rolling was definitely not my cup of tea. Imagine my joy when I discovered a flyer in my local library advertising Tai Chi, and local to boot! I joined up and soon got into the swing of things.

The teacher was quite receptive to my questions at first, but after a while my curiosity began to annoy him. He once said to me that when he had asked questions of his master, his master would hide what it was he was looking for and this had made him look more carefully and thoughtfully. I wondered how he could talk to me in such a way as if I didn't know what I was looking for. For how on earth could I find it with out help and guidance? This was where we parted company. This style was not for me. It was around this time there was an article on Tai Chi in the Telegraph which I read, and at the end of the article there was a phone number. A couple of phone calls later I was organised in Mark and Jenny Peters' class in Selly Oak. The Kai Ming (open minded) style of the club was completely different from that of the previous teacher and the class atmosphere open and warm.

Being a Nurse/Midwife I have a bad back as a result of lifting! I was looking for something which would not aggravate this old injury but would give me some physical benefits. (I was banned from yoga years ago!). I was also looking for something Martial after a particularly threatening incident on the streets during my community midwifery allocation, and most of all I was wondering about the breathing and how I could perhaps apply this to my work.

Some of our first lessons were spent walking! We walked up and down our hall forwards and backwards. We did exercises to learn about balance and changing weight. The focus of all the exercises and the lessons was the form. Mark said that while it may seem odd learning walking and breathing, (after all don't we do this naturally!) we would see gradual changes and sure enough I did. One incident happened when I was holding a baby for a mother. The baby was crying. I went into auto-pilot rocking the little soul into sleep. Then I realised I had been doing one of the warm up rocking exercises. Another occasion I was removing furniture and found myself walking backwards the Tai Chi way, transferring weight and so on and so forth! The list goes on.

The one thing that eluded me for some time though was the breathing. To have a better understanding of what this was all about I signed up for a Qigong workshop. Suddenly things seemed to fall into place, the diaphragm breathing to the dantien focus and relaxation was something I had been teaching in my childbirth classes but whereas Tai Chi remains with this pattern, the breathing style I had been teaching changes with progress in labour. I have come to feel that the original style I was teaching may not be as beneficial and I have changed the style of breathing and relaxation as a result of my Tai Chi experience. In my own private life I use the breathing when in situations of extreme stress, such as driving down the wrong motorway in the wrong direction when the kids are waiting to be picked up, or being catapulted up into the bright blue yonder as part of a gliding experience, and first day in a new job and so on. The qigong calms me down, enables me to focus, relax and so get through whatever stress I perceive at the time. I don't think I can say I'm a truly calm person, or have found that inner self that goes with calm, but qigong enables me to keep some kind of equilibrium.

With the passage of time I have discovered the muscles in my knees which sometimes ache after Tai Chi. Jenny and Maria have both noticed my knees turning or rather collapsing in. This is a major area of work for me as it is for many others. However I have found that overall my posture is better, my back aches less. Moving through as much form as I know loosens me up and enables me to face the challenges of the day.

The thing I like about the classes and why I keep going back for more is that questions are always welcomed, nothing is hidden. Martial applications are explained and demonstrated which is helpful to understand what it is I am doing. Not just a graceful move to keep my joints and bones well oiled but a punch and kick or some such other move which may be useful some day. I have joined other full day workshops which have enabled me to concentrate on different areas of Tai Chi for which there is no time in a regular class. I find these days are especially boosting though each time I realise how little I know and how much I still have to learn.

Something I have not mentioned till now but is no less important is the social aspect of the Tai Chi club. Over the year I have been going to Selly Oak and the workshop days I have met many people from different walks of life who all practice Tai Chi, all at different levels, all willing to help me when I am stuck or cannot remember something, all friendly, warm and accepting. All these elements add up to a very satisfying and complete experience, and I like to think that I have taken the first step towards long term improved health.

"The issuing energy starts in the root travels through the ankle, up to the knee, turned by the waist and manifested through the fingers.

Cheng Man Ching (1947)

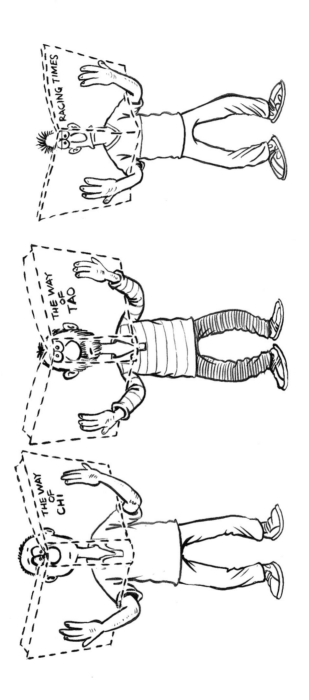

13

The Importance of Weapons Training in Tai Chi Chuan

Many students come to Taiji and believe all there is to the art is a slow form they've seen in the parks or on the TV. There is much, much more; it's a complete system including strengthening exercises, sensitivity exercises, philosophy and weapons. Different schools have various numbers of weapons but generally they all teach the straight sword (Jian). The reasons for this article is to explain their importance and the function of each weapon in their formation of the 'Taiji whole picture'.

I have known schools that teach weapons as a kind of dance; an extra bolt on to make their system more interesting and lucrative. Let's consider the dictionary definition for weapon – *an instrument of offence or defence* (the Wordsworth concise English dictionary); I suppose an extremely bad dance could be construed as '*offensive*' but I don't think they're quite the same thing.

Different weapons develop different skills or areas of Tai Chi Chuan; although our school practices straight sword, broad sword, walking stick, staff, spear and fan, I will focus on the most popular three to give a common ground. These are broad sword, spear and straight sword. These are sometimes referred to as the 100 day, 1000 day and 10,000 day weapons respectively, due to their level of complexity to master. I will explore each in turn.

Broad-sword (Dao)

We practice the 32 step Yang style form as described in Weapons of Primordial Pugilism by Dr. Tseng Ju-Pai. The blade is curved and single edge thereby making it a hacking and slashing weapon. There are two types readily available: a light flimsy one used by Wu Shu stylists and a more robust one favoured by Tai Chi Chuan (plus other northern Chinese martial art styles). As well as the solo form, individual training exercises are used along with partner work for application practice. This weapon uses coiling and extensively trains the waist as the power is needed to draw the blade through flesh or body (please try not to kill any partners in class). This was ostensibly a battlefield weapon but this does not mean it was designed to be wielded and applied as if you are in an Errol Flynn swash-buckling movie; It is important to use the skill of Tai Chi i.e. sticking, neutralising, redirecting and applying. When blocking a strike this should be done in a sweeping action and with the side of the blade to prevent damage to the cutting edge (the steel wasn't very good quality) in addition to the use of force against force. The circular force developed by this weapon is excellent for use in fixed step push-hands, grappling or throwing.

In terms of modern application the methodology could be applied to almost anything from the new police batons to an umbrella, walking stick or rolled up newspaper. The techniques can be applied empty hand against empty hand, or empty hand against a weapon to allow resistance training. In addition to this, heavy weapons improve strength and stamina; Yang Cheng Fu is quoted as saying "The heavier the weapons the more energies are gained". This is probably the most apt weapon for modern day as it is a close quarters weapons and includes seizing your opponent. It is extremely useful in developing Peng Jing (ward-off energy), the first and most important underlying energy used in Tai Chi Chuan

It is imperative that awareness of the weapon is developed, as both an extension of the body and improvement of focus. Be aware of the cutting edge as it slices through the air, of the hilt and pommel as striking implements in their own right; hitting with the butt of the weapon (pommel) is a very painful point strike as well as a method of creating space for the blade to cut through. Wrist locks can also be practiced with this section of the weapon and applied to everyday items, even a coke bottle (most likely not a 3 litre plastic one). We only have to look at Aikido to witness the effectiveness of weapons awareness applied effectively in empty hand techniques.

Spear (Qiang)

The spear is an excellent strength building weapon and I remember being told stories of practitioners thrusting the tip into heavy sacks and attempting to throw them away to build this power. A tale regarding the spear was told of Yang Ban Hou, Yang Cheng Fu's brother, who it was said, ordered the heads be removed from spears after his daughter was killed during spear play.

The most simple and common introduction to spear training is that purported to have been taught by Yang Cheng Fu and is commonly known as *shaking*. This involves three or four movements, dependent on how you count: (1) swing the head and tassel of the spear anti-clockwise by turning your waist and wrist and draw a circle. (2) swing the head and tassel of the spear clockwise by turning your waist and wrist and draw a circle. (3) thrust the spear forwards sliding it through your left hand. (4) pull back and press down. The first two movements are blocks and the third a strike. *Although simple these movements are fundamental to correct use of the spear*.

From here you can build on to two person spear work and form training. I have been taught a form developed by my teacher, Master Tan Ching Ngee of Singapore, which I find quite aerobic. The extended focus and footwork is ideal for developing advancing and entering skills. The use of Ting Jing and Fa Jing are apparent and the feeling of energy extension can be compared to form postures such as double push, single whip or left and right toe kick. Two person practice should have the flavour of push hands not of Friar Tuck and Robin Hood!! Techniques to consider are thrusting, controlled deflection and redirection to enter.

The use of same weapon and mixed weapon training/sparring will develop empty hand skills as well as weapons awareness. The ability to coil through an opponents attack and strike at their 'very heart' is a skill especially developed by the extension quality of the spear. It is said that the red horse hair is used to distract an attacker or their horse (it probably doesn't have the same effect with a car so don't try). It is also said that the hair is to stop blood dripping down the spear shaft and making the user lose grip; I've never put this to the test as you tend to lose students when you stab them ...

Straight-sword (Jian)

'Alive hold the sword, dead hold the sabre'. This Chinese saying means that the Broad-sword is rigid and inflexible whereas the straight sword is lively and flowing.

We practice the 54 step form as taught by Professor Cheng Man Chi'ng; this is my teacher's favourite weapon. We also practice the 13 sword secrets form, developed by Master Tan, to allow us to focus on the essential methods and hand grips used in proper Jian practice. This has long been considered the gentleman's weapon and it has been said that a scholar has to be well-read, and well-versed in fencing. The flavour of sword application is similar to that used in calligraphy; the smooth flow and sweeps require a skillful and light sensitive grip. It is apparent this weapon requires the highest level of skill and as such is often referred to in Chinese Mythology highlighting its importance in their culture. Nigel Sutton referred to this in his book 'Applied Tai Chi' where he compares it to the legend of Excalibur. These swords were often called 'Bao Jian' (precious sword). He stated that Professor Cheng is said to have owned such a sword and was able to pierce holes in coins.

Robert Smith quotes Professor Cheng as saying, "Never put more than four ounces on your opponent and never allow them to put more than four ounces on you". This principle is essential for proper Jian use; to sense your opponent's intentions and to offer him nothing is the highest skill in Tai Chi Chuan. Cheng, as with my teacher, lit up at the thought of sword sparring; this sparring is not swash buckling, it has the flavour of free push hands. The combination of Ting Jing and swift footwork are devastating in action.

The double edged sword is designed to be razor sharp at the tip and be progressively blunter towards the hilt as the blade thickens. This tapered thickness allows for a spring-like quality, as with Peng, and reduces the risk of the opponent finding your centre. It is designed to stick and deflect lightly then slash swiftly at vulnerable areas e.g. ankle tendons or thumbs. Sparring brings a new life to the weapon and in turn your empty hand techniques. The most apparent skill developed would be fast effective footwork which is essential for quick and effective combat. Moving from standard push-hands to striking is a natural progression developed by straight sword methodology.

A notable characteristic of the straight sword is the form of the free hand. This is held with the index and middle finger extended and the ring and little fingers bent and held by the thumb. This is commonly known as 'secret sword hand' and some say is used for striking vital points, in fact one exponent states that it is used to conceal a knife. A more practical interpretation is that it is used to balance the body and focus the chi; the whole body must have Yin and Yang, full and empty, and therefore no life in the other hand would break the principles of Tai Chi Chuan.

Each weapon develops essential Tai Chi skills and highlights them for correct use in all areas of this wondrous, multi-faceted art. The many energies including sticking, neutralising, understanding, redirecting and applying, find their place. Search out a teacher who knows and can apply the weapons, not just hang them on a wall. 'How to find a good teacher' is an article in the writing (watch this space) but initially follow a few simple rules:

1. research the art

2. ask their background, teachers etc.

3. check if they are members of the relevant governing body –

for Tai Chi it is the BCCMA and TCUGB

4. test their knowledge and application.

5. Or just pay me … !

"Be humble and not hesitate to ask those who may be lesser than you are."

Confucius

Professor Li De Yin with Kai Ming students in China shows Tai Chi sword

14

Kai-Ming Trip to China

People seemed surprised that I was going on holiday to China for a fortnight, until I explained that having been training in Tai Chi for some eight years , here was a chance to see first hand the country of its origin. It was to be a whirlwind of sightseeing, shopping and yes, we even managed to fit in some Tai Chi!

We arrived at Beijing airport after a nine hour flight and a change of plane at Paris, and were immediately plunged into a teeming mass waiting to exit the airport and reclaim their baggage. This was just an indication of how busy a city like Beijing can be. After a traditional Chinese breakfast of pork dumplings and rice porridge washed down by green tea we set out to experience the mayhem that is Beijing's traffic system. There was a visit to Tianamen square, in a 16-seater mini-bus that we were to spend almost as much time in as our hotel. The square itself was massive, and was teeming with people, showing no signs of the previous civil protests that brought it to the attention of the world.

To one side of the square was an enormous clock which was counting down to the millennium. While to the south a gigantic portrait of chairman Mao gazes down over the meridian gate, entrance to the forbidden city. Here we spent three and a half hours, with the expectation, what were we going to do with all that time? Of course we needn't have worried, as we worked our way across the city to the exit gate, and soon realised that if we didn't hurry up we were going to run out of time and miss something. As it was, we ended up rushing to see the last few halls which all had magnificent names such as "hall of great harmony" and " hall of preserving harmony" and were the most incredible sight of colour, detail and architecture, It was then time for lunch, which were always sumptuous feasts of nine or ten

dishes and over the course of the next fortnight we were to try just about every possible combination of Chinese food, including snake!

The afternoon was spent sightseeing around Beihai park, which has a lake, in the middle of which is a small island dominated by a white pagoda (temple) erected as a monument to the Dalai Lama's visit in 1651. The rest of the park comprises pavilions, temples and covered walkways. Particularly attractive is a painted gallery which arcs around the edge of the lake and looked splendid on the bright and sunny day on which we visited but again we were on borrowed time as we had to be back at the mini-bus for our next stop on the agenda, the friendship store, the first of many shopping expeditions.

The next day was to be the first day of training with Mrs. Dong a lady in her fifties (I think) who was going to teach us a Qigong set. First she took us through some warming up exercises where she proved she was considerably more flexible than some of us who were a lot younger. The form we were shown is practiced by vast numbers of Chinese every morning and I even saw it on breakfast TV, a sort of Chinese Mr. Motivator if you like! The form itself although not too long was more of an aerobic style, lots of stretching and twisting, but I'm afraid without the prompting of a video I don't think any of us would be able to remember the whole thing. Next we headed off to the Olympic village, where we had a special arrangement to look at the stock of martial arts weapons, which were somewhat cheaper than elsewhere. In fact they did quite well out of us, as I don't think too many people had seen such an array of weapons in one place before. We then finished the day off with a live buffet!

A meal not for the squeamish, as you unceremoniously dumped living crayfish into boiling water; the seafood doesn't come much fresher! The next few days were very similar. We got up at 7.0. a.m., had breakfast and then set off for the university training hall where we then began training with professor Li De Yin who taught us the 32 step straight sword form. Though it is difficult to remember a whole form in only two days, I hope to pick it up again when we get the video. Lunch was in the university canteen, which was an experience in itself as I have never attempted to eat spaghetti with chopsticks before!! In the evening we went to see a performance by the Peking opera which was very colourful but perhaps it wasn't such a good idea to stay drinking in the hotel bar till 1.0.a.m. as we had to be up at 7.15 a.m. for more training. Ouch!

We were extremely lucky to be taught by the professor as he is one of the foremost Tai Chi teachers in China , and although he spoke little English, he made sure through his son in law Taryo, who was with us from England, that we understood everything and spent a lot of time with us including the visits we made to the Chen family village and Shaolin temple at Henan. Our next couple of days meant, with our serious training out of the way, that we could get down to some serious sightseeing which included the Summer Palace, an antiques market, Temple of Heaven and the Thirteen Tombs, actually not that interesting, I'm afraid, but the following morning was our big day. We were going to get up at 5.0. a.m. in the morning and go down to the park and show them what we were made of. We attracted quite a lot of interest as we stumbled our way through the 32 step sword form and then joined in the 24 step Yang short form , which of course nobody knew either... But then it came to our choice and we demonstrated our form, which had never been seen before, as they had never even heard of Cheng Man Ch'ing. It was then time to leave and head off to a clothes market where everything was incredibly cheap or even counterfeit; you are never quite sure, nevertheless I managed to buy various items for myself and others back home.

The following day was a day I think we all had been waiting for as it was the trip to the Great Wall. It did not disappoint, although for some people proved a bit daunting as it gets quite steep in places. From the wall there are magnificent views, which unfortunately were spoiled a little by the misty conditions which were prevalent on the day we visited. Of course being one of the most famous landmarks in the world it was quite crowded, so we soon had to leave and return to our hotel to pack in readiness for our overnight train journey to Henan province to see the Shaolin temple and Chen family village. The actual train ride was not as bad as we had anticipated, although for a six footer like myself you do end up sleeping in one direction only, with your feet hanging over the end of the bed. Sharing an open compartment with five other people is a bit of a lottery but we managed to stay pretty well together, and I think I even managed to get some sleep.

In the morning, after breakfast at the Red Coral hotel we took a two hour coach ride to Shaolin but first paid a visit to the Forest of Pagodas. This is a resting place for all the master monks, which is a surprisingly pleasant place only spoiled by the sound of disco music drifting in from the market stalls outside. After spending a short time looking around the graveyard we then went to the Shaolin temple. This was somewhat smaller than I had imagined, and was somewhat lacking in the saffron robed figures whom I guess I was expecting. I think we all agreed we would have liked to spend more time here than we had been allowed and were soon whisked off to

Kai Ming students training in the extensive parks in China

Martin training in Push Hands

the dining room for our lunch, which was a fairly simple meal as compared to previous banquets. Then it was time to visit the local kung-fu schools, some of which have two thousand pupils. We were told they are basically taught Maths, English and kung-fu. The regime of the teaching staff seemed very strict, and if a pupil made a mistake or was not paying attention he was literally physically hit, until he performed perfectly. Next stop was another shopping expedition where at the market stalls a couple of us found the benefit of bartering and as I remember at least five of us bought another straight sword for a ridiculously cheap fifty yuan which is about four pounds.

The next few days were spent in more temples and friendship shops. By now we were just about overdosed on Chinese temple roofs, which are incredible to start with, but after a few hundred you start to feel a little jaded! So it was time for a change at the Longmen caves. These are literally carved out of a rock cliff, and are famous for the cave of ten thousand Buddhas, literally small Buddhas carved out of the rock all over the ceiling and walls, although I don't think we were there long enough to count them. After dinner we decided to venture forth to Beer city, a bar we happened upon, where we were welcomed with open arms. It may have been the fact the place was empty and they had karaoke night on, although Bora's brother Borak was the only one game enough to volunteer. He even gave us an encore! Well it was up again at 7.30 a.m., hangover and all, and off to the Chen family village which was a two hour coach journey away.

On the way some brave souls sampled the delights of the local latrines, gents and ladies! Although for myself, again being a six footer was a definite disadvantage and modesty prevented me from overlooking what was simply two ramshackle brick cubicles with a gully running away to a ditch. We have the pictures, please send cheques to the above address to acquire the negatives!!! When we finally arrived at the Chen training hall, we were asked to pay 50 yuan each for what turned out to be a half hour demo of hand and sword forms and some pushing hands demonstrations. Four of our instructors then boldly got up and demonstrated our form; needless to say we didn't charge them! Nuff said!

After the compulsory Tai Chi tourist shots outside, we had a short walk to Chenjiagou village to visit the house of Yang Luchan, where it is said while working as a servant he secretly spied on his master teaching and practising Tai Chi. When found out, master Chen Changxing was so impressed he agreed to take him on as a student. This was unheard of, as up until then Tai Chi was only passed on to family members. We then saw the enclosed graveyard of the past teachers and masters. They didn't seem to be held in the same reverence by some of the local children as perhaps it was by us foreign Tai Chi students, visiting the place of for the first time. They clambered and climbed over the walls to see what was going on. It was then time to get going again, past the monkey nuts drying in the sun, which was it seems the main local source of income. Although when Wilf offered to buy some he got more than he bargained for, expecting a small bag full he ended up with virtually a sack full and was trying palm them off on anybody and everybody for the rest of the day.

On the evening we were to meet for dinner with the local Wu-shu association representatives which did not, I am afraid go according to plan, as our party was split into two rooms. This was one of the only real problems we encountered on the entire holiday, and spoiled an otherwise pleasant meal. The following morning was yet another early start,. morning call at 5.25 a.m. catch the train back to Beijing at 7.20 a.m. for the seven hour journey back. The rest of the day spent on a Chinese puzzle? How do you put all the souvenirs and swords and clothes and everything else bought over the previous fortnight in one suitcase? Somehow we managed, with a ball of string to tie everything together, which left just the farewell dinner with Professor Li De-yin and his daughter, to whom I apologise for not naming but I could not get pronounce it correctly. We were given sterling service by her arranging all the memorable meals at restaurants of every conceivable variety. I thank her on behalf of everybody once more. At this point I should also give a mention to Mr Yu our driver without whom we would not have got to half the places we did do in our little mini-bus. He had little English, but was always smiling, certainly more punctual than some of his passengers!

As we left the Lan Bao Yuan hotel for the last time, I think we were ready for a rest after two weeks of continually being on the go. Many thanks should go to Tary Yip for his excellent organisation and translating, as very few mishaps occurred, and we always seemed to get where we wanted to be without too much trouble. It was a very enjoyable holiday and an experience I will treasure for years to come, and certainly one I hope to repeat in the not too distant future.

The present has not completely replaced the past ...

Heaven is long-enduring and earth continues long. The reason why heaven and earth are able to endure and continue thus long is because they do not live of, or for, themselves. This is how they are able to continue and endure.

Therefore the sage puts his own person last, and yet it is found in the foremost place; he treats his person as if it were foreign to him, and yet that person is preserved. Is it not because he has no personal and private ends, that therefore such ends are realised?

The J. Legge translation of the Tao Te Ching

15

Orlando '94

There I was at Gatwick airport, with hoards of holiday-makers, on my way to Orlando. They're all off to see Disney, Universal Studios, Sea World and the rest. What am I going to be doing? I'll be with my fellow British team mates competing in the *1994 UNITED STATES NATIONAL CHINESE MARTIAL ARTS COMPETITION* at the Marriott World Centre Resort.

We're all back now, and victorious to-boot!!

There were ten of us making up the British team and we jointly won eight gold's, twelve silver's and three bronze medals. The competition lasted three days, being 3rd, 4th & 5th September, but we all stayed on for a few days. Well, you can't go to Orlando and not see Mickey Mouse!

Peter Young organised the team, via the TCUGB, which consisted of myself, Garry, Steve Burns, Alan McDonnell (an instructor from Leigh) and Peter plus some of his students. There were approximately 1000 competitors and 100 judges, of which Peter was one, and the whole event was awash with famous teachers. I was personally grateful for the opportunity to meet William CC Chen and Yang Jwing Ming.

The underlying feeling to the whole event was one of friendship and openness. Too many of these such occasions end up with schools sticking to their little groups not wanting to get too friendly with their "competitors". This was far from the situation here; in fact when it came to the full-contact competition I was asked to wrap a Brazilian team member's hands, by their coach, even though one of his team was up to fight Steve Burns, the Zhong Ding student who was fighting for Great Britain. Steve went on to win the Silver medal for his weight category. William Chen told us he was impressed with this result as Steve was the only Tai Chi exponent taking part in the event. As most people, who know of Mr. Chen, are aware he himself has previously entered and won such a competition; this is documented in Robert Smith's book, *Chinese Boxing, Masters & Methods*.

The event included internal and external Chinese arts, both weapons and empty hand. It was especially gratifying to see the children's events and to appreciate the effort they put in as well as the skill level they had obtained.

This was also the first time I had seen the soft weapons sparring developed by Adam Hsu. Just before we set out for Orlando I had read an article in *Inside Kung-Fu* which made it look interesting and fun, so I entered. I am very pleased to say I won a silver medal. Initially I thought it might end up like Escrima with rubber sticks, but I am happy to say a concerted effort on the part of the referee and judges prevented this happening. The swords came complete with rubber hilt and pommel; strikes were only scored if they were performed with proper cut¬ting action or strong stab. Just hitting was discounted, as was randomly waving the weapon around in a sort of "web of death". I can see this taking off in a big way in Britain; in fact Peter said he intended introduce it at his competition in 1995. Coincidentally I entered Peter's event and won gold. Garry won two silvers in push-hands for his weight category and I won two golds for push-hands, one silver and one bronze for forms, and one silver for weapons sparring. The standard was good and the number of entrants high. William Chen told Garry and me that he was impressed with us and we have since been considering bringing him to the UK as Cheng Man Ch'ing's most senior living disciple. Quite a few Americans were jealous of the amount of attention he was showing us.

16

Due to Requests, Here Are the Requirements for Senior Instructor Grade:

- Ability to spell Tai Chi Chuan correctly

- Legs resembling tree trunks

- Waist must exceed inside leg measurement by at least 16"

- An advantage to have thin or receding hair (makes Mark feel better)

- Obsessive to the extent that your partner has left you (you will then be more available to run errands for Mark or Garry).

- Paid excessively for private lessons with a chief instructor, even though most of it was spent in standing post while he watched Kung Fu movies.

- Must have been slammed into the floor (like a good 'un) by a chief instructor and heard to cry, "God he's fast, I didn't even see that coming".

- Must never have pushed a chief instructor over as it may show them all up for the frauds they are.

- Gaze in awe daily at your framed photo of Garry & Mark, hung over your bed.

- Never question anything they say; if you do not understand, presume you're stupid.

- Must own at least 50 Tai Chi related books (bought from the club)

- Must have sold at least 1 copy of each Kai Ming video to every student in your class. Better still, 2 copies (1 for spare).

- Oh yes, and know the whole syllabus so you could be tested on 'You Bet'

Alternatively, a limited number of grades could be purchased with a significant bribe ...

PATENT PENDING!!!!!!!!

A recent invention has been proposed, by a member of the student body, to aid in practice of the form. It has been noted that training aids such as books and videos are all very well, but you have to keep referring back or looking over your shoulder.

WELL NOT ANY MORE ...

Above are development sketches provided by Irvine Porter. There are two versions, standard and deluxe. Prices are yet to be confirmed, but we will no doubt be looking for guinea pigs for field trials.

The standard model comes complete with suction page turner and optional helmet light.

The deluxe model has a built in video player and black and white monitor. We are considering a super-deluxe model, which will include a camera to review your progress and a colour monitor with TV program capability.

WATCH THIS SPACE ...

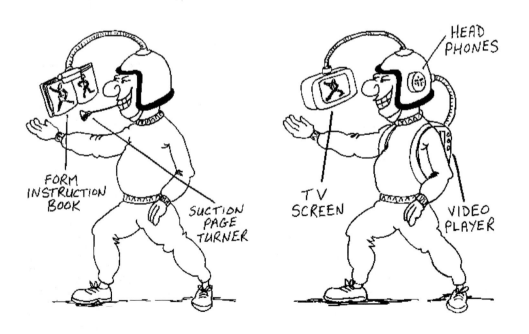

FORM INSTRUCTION BOOK

SUCTION PAGE TURNER

HEAD PHONES

TV SCREEN

VIDEO PLAYER

17

M.A.D.

I am writing on behalf of the wives and girlfriends of men afflicted by Martial-Arts **A**ddictive Dementia, commonly known as 'M.A.D.'; the symptoms of which can be varied and extremely upsetting to the sufferer's carer. They include such things as:

- Involuntary movements of the hands and arms, which as the disease progresses can appear at any time and are known by the term 'Blocks'; similar forceful jerking of the legs has also been observed

- Some of the afflicted have a tendency to utter a loud cry as these movements take place, described by some as a 'whoop'.

There are clubs 'M.A.D.' sufferers can attend, up to seven days a week depending on the degree of addiction, where they can discuss their disease and try in pairs or groups to coordinate their involuntary movements and use them to their advantage, usually as some simple form of self-defence! They have their own magazines, by which they can keep in touch with their own kind, and spend hour after hour gleaning every small scrap of information from these, which may help them to understand and develop their dementia, which is regarded by the most severely afflicted as an 'Art Form'. The words Chen, Yang, Kung Fu and Chi appear to evoke great excitement when introduced into their conversation. Karate, Judo, Aikido, Wing Chun, there are many variations of 'M.A.D.', but Tai Chi Ch-uan

"WHY DON'T YOU GO OUTSIDE AND PRACTICE THAT?"

with the well-known terribly afflicted sufferer Mark Peters seems the most addictive, with its slow (almost hypnotic) movements.

At the present time no treatment is available, and I feel the partners of the addicts need some form of support group, therefore perhaps if the response is great enough, I would be willing to arrange a twenty-four hour help line to cater for certain times of crises for these people, such as over-doses (weekend camps) and video nasties (Enter the Dragon, Hard to Kill, etc).

As the partners of these men suffer sexual deprivation, because of the 'M.A.D.' addicts' constant 'high', I will probably also arrange trips to male strip clubs, and hopefully see the Chippendales in action. My in-depth knowledge of this disease stems from a close association with a sufferer whom I will refer to as Kato (remember the Pink Panther?) His greatest joy is to stand poised on the patio, in the moonlight, freezing cold, with a broom handle held majestically aloft (I think this represents a broad sword). The feeling he gets as he stands shuddering with hypothermia is the nearest he will ever get to mingling Chi with the likes of Cynthia Rothrock.

Therefore, I hope you will publish my letter and enable me to help other carers realise they are not 'forgotten people'.

18

What's in an Experience?

Experiential understanding is the understanding of truth. Anything else is apparent understanding. If I spend hours studying history I well may become a learned man. I will 'know' so much and yet I will not know the truth of any of the information because facts and dates cannot give true experience of anything.

What is experienced can be related to others but the experience cannot be given. If we want to give somebody an experience then all we can do is give guidelines which relate to our own experience. An example is a friend wants to learn to swim but is a little frightened. I am keen to help. I say how wonderful it is to glide though the water and that there is nothing to fear

I want to give them the experience of swimming. I introduce them to water and then demonstrate how to swim. Whilst learning to swim my friend will experience a similar experience which I had while learning but it will not be the same experience and my experience whilst teaching my friend to swim is very different from my friend's experience of learning.

I am relaxed and confident of my ability and safety; my friend is entering into a scary activity; he has to put his trust in me and he will also feel self conscious and at times frustrated when he can't do it. With practice he improves and learns to swim. He will develop his own way of swimming which suits him. If he becomes very keen on swimming he may go to a coach who will teach him how to improve his technique. My friend has learned something of the truth of swimming.

Another friend becomes very interested in swimming and having watched a swimming gala goes to the library and finds a book on Olympic swimming

champions. He reads it and becomes fascinated by the whole subject of swimming history. He furthers his reading learning all the secrets of the great coaches of swimming. He becomes an expert on swimming and he knows so much about swimming. The three of us sit watching a swimming race on TV my first friend and I are astounded by our friend's knowledge; we feel humbled as he explains how the winning swimmer has used a particular variation of a stroke to win the race. My first friend is eager to try this technique and asks our expert who confidently demonstrates the intricacies of the movement; how the wrist and elbow turn with the hip and so forth. We suggest going swimming the next day so that we can test it in the water our friend; the expert cannot make it, it seems he's allergic to water.

We can all become knowing without experience. I know the form because I learned how to do somebody else's movements and copied them; I received verbal instruction in order to understand what I should be feeling and I read books on the subject to further my understanding. My experience and exposure to different teachings has taught me to discriminate more clearly, to feel whether a position is physiologically correct rather than taking other peoples word for it. In push hands our experience of the activity can only be the truth of the moment, however the nature of pushing hands means that while we may be practising the activity we are not really present with the truth of feeling.

If we are to really gain insight into our sensitivity then we have to access a subtler level of truth. This truth is that how we react in push hands may not be the truth in terms of developing martial ability. An example, I push hands with a smaller lighter partner and they start to push and I start to turn the waist to neutralize, my partner's push is partially deflected so he is now in a weaker position. I then use a small amount of effort to complete the deflection and my partner is uprooted. I have failed to listen and invest in loss; I have 'won'. I take this ability into a sparring situation and find I get hit a lot and can't work out why. The reason is that I an not prepared to experience being moved; I cannot let my ego rest I have to find some immediate gain in what I am doing. In order to gain self defence skills from Tai Chi which is taught with the emphasis on developing these skills in push hands then you have change your perception of success.

In a pushing hands competition two competitors go hell for leather. We see some spectacular skills; one man seems on the brink of defeat, about to be pushed out but with great determination and a strong root he stops and then uses his opponent's desperate lunge to put him off balance. The man flies through the air and there is great applause. We have seen a champion of pushing hands at work. The same man enters a fighting competition; he is punched senseless and cannot work out why. The skill which enabled him to root and manipulate his opponent out of an area had taught him to defend positions that cannot be defended when the dynamic of the activity changes.

An arm which is trying to push you has a very different dynamic from one that is trying to punch you. This man's pushing hands did not inform his self defence skill. If we want to develop self defence skills from pushing hands then we must not manipulate our partner in order to stop them moving our centre; we must develop the sensitivity to know (experience) when to enter and gain the upper hand through good structure and when to concede ground and withdraw in order to gain a better position. This knowledge alone would not prepare someone for a fighting competition. But if studied and practiced honestly then a person will have developed some physical intelligence, which will enable them to avoid using brute strength. At this subtler level of truth one must continually ask the question: am I truly feeling and responding to my partner or are other factors influencing my response? Is my status in the class such that I must win, at the other end of the spectrum of ego is my self esteem so low that I lose my structure and never gain the advantage, or I do I pride myself on some aspect of pushing hands such as yielding and so look only for opportunities to use this skill?

While evolving in the activity we may find that there are all sorts of reasons why we fail to pay proper attention and it is important not to become despondent about this or to judge yourself. This is self-cultivation, realising how your ego works not trying to suppress or ignore it. practiced correctly the practice of pushing hands can lead to a heightened understanding of and sensitivity to force; practiced incorrectly it will lead to self delusion and the use of excessive force. Not only must you experience the activity but also you must be aware of how you achieved the result, if you cause your partner to be put off balance then be aware of whether you had to use force to achieve the result, when you use structure and a relaxed non-striving approach the feeling is very different.

The skilful masters (of the Tao) in old times, with a subtle and exquisite penetration, comprehended its mysteries, and were deep (also) so as to elude men's knowledge. As they were thus beyond men's knowledge, I will make an effort to describe of what sort they appeared to be.

Shrinking looked they like those who wade through a stream in winter; irresolute like those who are afraid of all around them; grave like a guest (in awe of his host); evanescent like ice that is melting away; unpretentious like wood that has not been fashioned into anything; vacant like a valley, and dull like muddy water.

Who can (make) the muddy water (clear)? Let it be still, and it will gradually become clear. Who can secure the condition of rest? Let movement go on, and the condition of rest will gradually arise.

They who preserve this method of the Tao do not wish to be full (of themselves). It is through their not being full of themselves that they can afford to seem worn and not appear new and complete.

19

Tai Chi Waves

Over the years of assisting and teaching with my husband at his Tai Chi classes one of the most often asked questions by the students of this art has been. "So what should I be feeling when I practice the form?"

Most are at the stage where they have been training for a while and are now able to perform the whole form smoothly, and without having to stop at some point having forgotten the next move. By the time students reach this point, they want to be able to shift the focus of practice from, "Oh, dear that move didn't feel quite right", and maybe feel the benefits of improved postures and free flowing movements

Until a few weeks ago my standard reply after thinking initially about my own experiences within the years of my practice, was to tell them, "There is no right answer to this, what you feel from one week to another may change."

Most people comment on the relaxation and "feel good factor" the form work gives them, and is the reason most seek out a Tai Chi class in the first place. Some are happy to accept this new oasis of calm their practice gives them. Others as they progress on the Tai Chi journey want or hope to experience many things more. Now all thought it has taken me fifteen years of living and breathing the art (being the partner of a Principle instructor is not always a perk) I think I can answer the aforesaid enquiry in a perhaps more informed way, having what many call, "A breakthrough" or some less kindly perhaps comment, " What took you so long!"

Having learned the form myself, after some traumatic episodes where I really thought I would never remember the postures, I have always enjoyed the graceful moves and the feeling of achievement that I get when I perform the closing posture. There were times over the years when I really thought this

time would elude me. If I am honest I felt that this was enough. Many students don't even get through the first ten weeks of training. The Chen Man-Ch'ing form we practice is simplified, not simple, a quote from that great master, and many in this frantic world we live in find that if instant results cannot be achieved, it is easier to leave than persevere. What happened to the saying that, "Anything worth having takes patience and time to acquire"? I can understand their feelings.

Maybe if Mark had not bribed me with sums of money amounting to figures I am unwilling to disclose to help in the class each week, I may have gone the same way. Anyway as I said until a few weeks ago I was satisfied with where I was. I have heard my husband speak in class about letting the feeling of a wave flow through your body when running through the form. I had never really thought about this too much, but one evening at one of the regular classes we run I commenced Lift Hands, an opening move and thought let's give this "wave" a go! There is a saying in Tai Chi, "Where the mind goes the Chi follows," which I define as where the mind goes the focus goes, so I thought the best place to start the "wave" was at the fingertips. With each posture I focused on my hand, and as my shoulders relaxed, then my elbows I had a feeling of a wave of relaxation going through my muscles and spreading throughout my body. As I moved slowly through the form this pleasant experience continued. So that is what he's been talking about I thought as I finished. Now I try to achieve this each time.

Although my husband assures me I don't look like an octopus I sometimes liken the feeling I get to how the tentacles move. Almost as if something is travelling along them smoothly and silently. Cutting effortlessly through the water. Ah, if only! I can just about cope with co-ordinating four limbs let alone 8. Before I began Tai Chi, as a nurse I very often suffered high levels of stress and at one point tried listening to relaxation tapes. Problem was if you have ever tried this you will know that by the time you have taken the phone off the hook, put a do not disturb notice on the front door, shut the dog in the kitchen, turned off your mobile phone, set the tape up to run and managed to get that lumpy cushion in a comfortable area of your back the last thing you can do is relax your mind enough to listen to the flipping tape. You are thinking about all the important phone calls you might be missing, the dog is scratching the door to get to you, to the point that he's left half of his nails in it, and the woman next door is trying to peer through the curtains to see if you are in fact in and all right and what's going on that you don't want to be disturbed from!

I only once achieved my goal. This was done by closing the curtains downstairs, putting the tape on remote handset, and shutting the dog in the utility and giving him something to occupy his mind, a piece of chocolate in plain sight but too high for him to reach by jumping. I then sat in my recliner and as I felt the warmth that true relaxation brings spreading through my body I fell asleep and missed the important bits… Unfortunately I was soon bought back to reality by the dog, by now suffering from chocolate deprivation mania, taking one last desperate leap for the prize and sending the free standing vegetable rack crashing into the table and knocking the bottle of milk off it, on to the floor where it promptly broke. Now that I have discovered Tai Chi and the "wave" I can get the relaxation, the warmth, the feel good factor, and more importantly the dog no longer needs his therapist.

All this is available to anyone who starts their own Tai Chi journey. I cannot say how long it will take, or if they will ever get to the end, but the truth is it doesn't matter, just enjoy the ride!

In past history, if a scholar mastered a single subject, then others could study it from him. That scholar could then, as a teacher, connect the students with the sages of the past many years ago, a certain Cheng Kuan-wen was acknowledged as being widely knowledgeable and was dubbed san-chueh, having achieved excellence in three fields (poetry, calligraphy, and painting. Down the ages it has been lamented that there have been so few like him.

Now, Professor Cheng excelled in five fields: poetry, painting, calligraphy, and t'ai-chi ch'uan (a martial art), and medicine. He was famous the world over for these attainments. He also studied deeply the teachings of former sages, and was such a prolific writer that he did not realize old age was creeping upon him. Professor Cheng surpassed the accomplishments of Cheng Kuan-wen. People who believe him to be the most outstanding individual in Chinese cultural history in this century (literally, since the founding of the Republic of China, 1911) are not exaggerating.

Tam Gibbs – Cheng Tzu:
Master of the Five Excellences
A Life Biography of Cheng Man Ching

20

What Am I Doing?

"Stand there and push the other person over, but you can't use any force" and "Don't compete – it's best if you lose" or "Non-action and Invest in loss". Hmmm – easy, not! One of the main questions asked by student is "What am I doing?" What are they doing, if you haven't already guessed? Push hands. Even students of some years' practice can ask this seemingly easy question. One of my answers is "the form is getting to know yourself and push hands is to know somebody else", but this statement only scratches the surface. In external martial arts student usually have sparring sessions as I did back in my Wado Ryu and Lau Gar days. The question here is never asked it's obvious, it's fighting. If it were asked I would like to think it would be answered more or less the same way. We learn the form, exercises, skills, and other tools taken from the toolbox known as our style, what for? We all do martial arts and especially Tai Chi Chuan for individual reasons, but I believe the end result is the same in everyone. That is your confidence, general health and wellbeing can be greatly enhanced. This is because the principles, etiquette, etc, learnt while doing your style soon flows over into other areas in your life. This should be true of push hands and even sparring.

It is interesting to watch someone push for the first time you can almost feel the conflict within the person. This manifests itself in various ways. Two of those ways, which seem most frequent, are either they will not attempt to anything at all and want to stop or they will try and obliterate the other person. Both having the desired result in not having to deal with the idea of pushing. I suppose it's part of our fight or flight mechanism kicking in. If the person persists with this intangible pursuit you can see the confidence levels rise. They still may have no idea what they are doing, but they are doing it and once this initial barrier is overcome then they can start to understand push hands. It should not be competition, winning or losing, but learning. If a student is only thinking about winning or losing then their minds are closed to all the other possibilities.

The same focus used in the practice of the form should also be used in pushing. The principles should be adhered to without exception. What is the point in learning the forms and foundations of your art so that when you go to use it you throw it out the window? You don't learn to drive your car and then push it everywhere. Sometimes when pushing with new students you do feel as if each time you step up to push that you could just push straight through them uprooting them with ease, but this would prove nothing. Yes, there may be a time and place when this would be acceptable, but not with beginners. If you are free pushing with a partner and you are able to uproot them it should have been done with the smallest amount of force and thought. You and your partner should have had no idea of what was coming. The idea is that you are only really interested in following the flow of the energy and keeping to the principles. What usually happens is that when the other person is uprooted they have actually put themselves off balance by following the force into an area that they are not happy with. At a higher level you should be aware of openings which you could take advantage of. The trick is to wait for the openings and only take advantage if there is little or no opposing force. All the movements should be spontaneous – this conceals any intent. If you try to create openings your intentions would be known by your partner and used against you.

When you have learnt the form well enough it should be done as if you don't know what the next move is until you have done it and on to the next one. Your focus should be on the principles and not on thinking what comes next. The form and push hands are not that different and should be done with the same focus and intent. Exercises like Da lu are used to infuse the two ideas. In push hands there may be instances when you pull-put textbook movements from the form and while doing the form there maybe points where you go blank not knowing what to do next. When we go blank what happens? Nothing, this is because it is instilled that we do the form 100% accurately. Doing the form accurately is important, but not to the point that it makes the form stagnant. Try to do the form alone not really focusing on the moves to a point where you go blank, it may be hard at first, and turn it into push hands or go into a different form – the form then can become more flowing and flexible.

A better name for push hands is sensing hands. When you take part your focus should be on all the energies being used or not used as the case may be. One of these feelings that should be harnessed is when your partner becomes double weighted in their legs. The body, if properly relaxed, should be able to pick up on the differences as to when somebody is either double or single weighted. To feel the difference, get a partner to stand both double and single weighted and then push them around. When you are happy with this get your partner to push hands and change to double weightiness every now and then to see if you can sense the difference. No action is required – a simple verbal exchange will do to keep each side in form. Once this has been taken to a comfortable level, other areas can be worked on and explored.

Sometimes when I push with students they will push me into areas that they themselves get caught out on and they try to see what I do or ask 'what if?' questions. I suppose the general idea is that the instructors walk about with every scenario in his/her head. In fact, this would be impossible there would be too many variations and it would put an end to the movements being spontaneous. So usually the best way to explain is to make them aware of how they feel to the other person: uprooted, double weighted, etc, and usually comes down to what bit they need to relax. If you go through it blow by blow, and through what they did, that so I'll should do this I would be flat on my back. This is somewhat of a general account of push hands, but I hope it will help you up that first of many difficult steps and with a bit of practice and faith in the principles of Tai Chi Chuan the body will take care of itself.

21

There's more to this Tai Chi than just waving your hands about ...

In the mid 1970's, a new type of film was unleashed on the unsuspecting western world bringing with it a name that was to pass into legend. The film was "Enter the Dragon", and the star was a small Chinese-American by the name of Bruce Lee – and didn't we all want to be like him! To have the physique, the balance, the power and the sheer venomous speed of the guy, dispatching assailants with a blur of fists and feet. Along with Bruce Lee, two other terms entered into common usage in the western languages. These were Kung-Fu and Martial Arts.

Since then I've always admired people who practiced this new religion. Whilst at college in London, I used to travel to various training halls where the Sifu would put his students through their paces – sit-ups, crunches, press-ups, arm exercises, leg exercises, single forms, two man forms. I was knackered just watching them!

The Sifus were always very approachable, in fact if you met them in the street you wouldn't know they were martial arts experts. In the training hall though they looked, well, dangerous! They looked las though they could rip your throat out, whilst you were frozen like a wide eyed rabbit caught in the headlights of a 40 ton juggernaut. You could not help but admire them for the sheer training dedication and will power needed to attain these skills; not for the faint hearted or watery stomached.

So here I am, a beginner in the martial arts, standing at the back listening to and watching the instructor. But wait, something is wrong. I've been here several months and the words sit-ups and press-ups haven't even been mentioned. The instructor is a slightly shorter version of Billy Crystal and is twice as funny. He looks anything but dangerous. My mother would knock him out, and not break sweat.

But wait again! Fortunately I've seen a video of this chameleon of a chap demonstrating his Tai Chi Chuan , and he is dangerous, *very* dangerous! My instructor practices one of the soft or "internal" martial arts, compared to the hard or external styles, although there is definitely nothing soft about a palm in the face or ribs, or being thrown onto a concrete floor at one hundred m.p.h. The main observable difference between the hard and soft styles is that on looking around at my compatriots, there is a wide range of ages and shapes catered for, and none of them have bulging muscles or veins standing out on their necks. Why, even my mother, now demoted from knock-out specialist, could do it and enjoy it.

However, like any enterprise in life, the study of Tai Chi is a journey and requires commitment and a good map. The commitment comes from you. The sheer will power needed to get out of the chair after a hard day's work, take that long walk over to the television and press the off button, climb into the car and drive to the training hall. The commitment to turn up week in. week out, the commitment to practice at least sometimes on your own and the commitment to learn. The map is your instructor, who is going to guide you from point A, complete novice, to point B, and the good thing about a journey is that having reached point B and you really like it, well you can stay there, or if you wish, hopefully using the same map, you can go to point C. This map is very, very important, make sure it's a good one!

So when you're out looking for your instructor map, make sure that he or she can take you to where you want to go. In other words, can the map do the business? Not only that, can this talking map explain when going from A to B why you need to go in a certain direction? The point I'm trying to make here is that in the western world we're just not cut out to obediently follow a master, humbly standing in this stance, or that stance, not knowing why. We like asking questions and we like answers that make sense, and so should your map, make sense, otherwise …

- Now, I want you to go outside and lick the pavement clean with your tongue (well, what else would you lick it with?!).
- *Why?*
- Because it's the done thing.
- *No chance!*
- Okay, it's because the pavement needs cleaning.
- *No chance again!*
- In that case, it's because it'll develop iron tongue, and you'll be able to slay any adversary with one touch of your tongue – or what's left of it!
- *Now you're talking, where's that pavement?*

Important isn't it? And all the questions that you ask should be answered by your instructor in a sensible way, and not shrouded in mystery or fobbing you off.

So having attained a good map whom you're happy with, what else should you do? Well, that's easy, enjoy yourself and learn. You either enjoy something or you don't, but one of the nice things about Tai Chi is that you're immersed slowly into the aspects of it, one slowly blending with another which is easier for the body system to adapt to.

None of this – two lessons, now pad up and you're on to sparring with Crusher Smith over there.

- *But I don't know what I'm doing!*
- That's okay, neither does he, now don't forget – control!

And as you're led bleeding and concussed from the mat –

- A bit more control there Crusher, but showed good aggression, that's what we like to see – now about you.
- *Who me?* (Trying to focus on one of three shadowy figures).
- Good try, but let's see more aggression next time.
- *Next time! What next time?*
- In fact, let's keep you on the mat and see how you get on with Crusher's brother – Killer!

  Now where's he gone?!

No, in Tai chi, you're slowly immersed, drip fed, doing each stage with stabilisers, and all of a sudden realising that the stabilisers have been removed and you didn't even notice!

As you learn, you'll find out more about yourself, your balance, your co-ordination, your sensitivity, and once you can control these, you'll also find you'll be able to control someone who may wish to do you harm. So should Crusher Smith or his brother try to rob you or attack you – and I hope he never does – with your new found skills it should be he, and not you, looking in the mirror the next day looking like a negative of a panda and trying to re-straighten his nose.

But better still, should Mr. Smith manage to persuade the CPS to haul you into court claiming that your hands and feet are deadly weapons and should have been handed into the police in the 1997 armistice – you can in all innocence claim that you don't know what he's talking about, you only do Tai Chi, along with your sweet dear old mother!

So this is the start of my Tai Chi journey, my views from the back of the class. As I pass from place to place, I can always go back and re-examine what I think I've already learned, and learn some more, rather like re-reading a book, there's always something important I'll have missed.

Now do you want to watch EastEnders, or do you want to go on a journey to discover more about yourself? Go on, reach for the off button!

Professor (Cheng Man-ch'ing) used to say, "As you grow more relaxed, you become less afraid. And as you become less afraid you grow more relaxed."

Wolfe Lowenthal – There Are No Secrets

22

The Mystery of Mastery

The practice of martial arts is often cited as a path to self cultivation. The more esoteric the art the more this is emphasised. What evidence is there that martial training will lead the practitioner to become a master of himself? How can the training of fighting techniques lead to self improvement?

Most so called civilised people would agree that fighting/conflict/violence is undesirable and that an interest in fighting is brutish. If this is the case then it seems unlikely that someone who spends hour after hour perfecting techniques designed to cause injury to another person is a likely candidate to develop the attributes of compassion and love that are generally ascribed to cultivated human beings. The answer to this paradox may lie in the fact that the training of a martial artist asks very searching questions of that person's true nature. In order to develop insight and wisdom in their chosen art there is a need to put aside the baggage of their ego.

This emptying of the cup is a requirement of all spiritual disciplines.

On the whole it is doubtful whether many martial art schools do help to further the spiritual integrity of their students; in the main this is because the students' perception of what martial training involves has been coloured by its media image of flashy macho men defeating all-comers. Schools that cater for this type of 'modern' approach have a high profile and fit the image projected by the media. Most authentic schools find that many new students hope to achieve instant mastery and dislike hard work. Most beginners do not tend to stay long, especially if the art being taught does not offer some incentive to the ego. A shimmering silk suit and flashy techniques will attract more people than a plain white gi and repetitive training. The aim of this piece is not to lambast the charlatans who do not understand the true nature of training but to give an example of someone who does.

My example of a martial artist who has developed all the symptoms of a cultivated being is a very good friend of mine and who is a true Master of Karate. This man started training over thirty years ago. He admits to being lucky to have had a very serious and talented teacher. His teacher never gave him any quarter. He was his teacher not his friend. As he developed ability and achieved higher grades so his training became more exacting and at times humiliating. There was little time for philosophy; just train, don't think, train.

He became a good fighter. If an awkward student from another school turned up and was giving other people trouble then my friend got the job of demonstrating the effectiveness of his style. I first trained with my friend years ago and in one five-minute session he devastated me, my ego was reeling. I was a student of the greatest art in the universe, Tai Chi Chuan, my teacher was a world champion (of form) and I couldn't have hit this Karateka with a bag of rice, yet he could pick me off at ease. I went away battered without a physical mark on me. The knowledge that I had been so easily and gently dealt with was more devastating than any physical beating I have had. I had mistaken the words *grand ultimate boxing* for the name of a style. What a grand ultimate boxer understands is the experiential reality of boxing/fighting. Timing, distancing, relaxed power and above all else fearlessness.

The fighting skills alone cannot be cited as evidence of self cultivation, in fact there are many people who possess all the physical skills, and yet they behave with no regard or compassion for others; they are totally concentrated on destruction. When the mind is full of anger and is concentrated with bad intentions this makes for a formidable opponent. This type of martial artist rather than weakening the ego and developing humility becomes a terrible bully and hands down a legacy of meanness. This type of Master has not developed Wu de (martial virtue) The difference between a true martial arts Master/grand ultimate boxer and a mere martial arts fighter is in the development of what Buddhists call right concentration. Concentration with moral fibre.

Someone whose only initial aim is to be the best karateka finds that at some point a time comes when competing with others loses its appeal simply training for the sake of it and to develop understanding of the art starts to take over. During free sparring they notice how much more effective they become when the emotions are detached from the activity.

Pain is felt for what it is, a sensation, any emotional attachment to this pain (anger/fear) will cause loss of concentration. Any dwelling on mistakes (self consciousness) will detract from what is happening in the fight. As he becomes more attentive he finds that when sparring with lesser opponents he takes care of them. When fighting with skillful dangerous opponents he is able to engross himself in the activity. Without actively thinking about it the ego has taken a back seat. During form/Kata the mind is focused on his own body; again no time outs. Underlying it all is vigorous, exacting, harsh training. The ego does not like harsh training; it wants to check out, give in to the pain and take a rest.

Through externally imposed discipline an acceptance grows that there is no way out, the voice of the ego is shut out, the mind becomes clearer, the body relaxes, technique improves. The purpose is not the training of the body alone but of the body, mind and spirit. The martial artist is learning the art of life. Meanwhile over the street the mean machine is dispatching his hapless students to the local hospital. He is certainly the more impressive man because that's what his training has become – a means to impress; his concentration is born out of a fear of defeat and humiliation. My friend's training has without him necessary initially intending it to be become a method of self cultivation leading him to be comfortable with himself and the world. My friend's countenance is happy; he does not live in fear because he has studied and come to terms with something which lies at the heart of man's weakness, the fear of confrontation, violence, death.

Maybe the mean machine will also come to this realisation but first he will have to take a beating and realise that natural talent and dedication to winning at all costs is not enough, sadly too often they simply retreat into the cocoon of sycophantic students who push them onto a pedestal.

The martial way of Karate is different from Tai Chi and the emphasis on relaxation and developing an effortless economic physicality in Tai Chi is not through harsh training. So how can we claim that this art is for self-cultivation? Many students are content to simply follow their teacher's often untested methods. The world of Tai Chi is crammed with people who take themselves seriously and love to bicker and argue over some kind of surreal authenticity, claiming to be true descendants of this ancient school or that. Pushing hands can give us a chance to investigate our fears but all too often we simply use it as a method of being obstructive and manipulative.

A hard shove to the chest can be resisted (watch any pushing hands competition). Not so a hard punch to the jaw. One of the fascinations of the art is the huge cannon of literature on the subject. All too often this historical learning takes the place of real training leading to intellectualism, which can be a great hindrance to gaining insight. Tai chi without fighting training may still lead us on to the path of self-cultivation because self-cultivation does not have to be learned through fighting training. Being enlightened does not mean you have to be a skillful fighter or want to fight.

A Tai Chi player who becomes mindful through practice of form alone will be cultivating himself. The Tai Chi player who develops a competitive attitude in the safe practice of push hands and set partner exercises is not practising a 'way' and is only cultivating arrogance and ignorance. I know I've been there.

If I am pushed and lose my balance and I react by grabbing my partner and fighting not to lose my position or I use my ability to root with muscular strength to toss them around I may feel I have done o.k. I have manipulated my way out of defeat. In truth I have learned nothing. Because the sensations we get in pushing hands are subtle in comparison to being punched or kicked we can develop insensitivity to what is happening. Real understanding of timing and distance can be learned through the practice of push hands, because many teachers do not understand the method correctly; the students are left to push and shove or go insipidly through the motions. To be fearless is perhaps the key to being truly happy. As we walk the path gradually facing up to whatever our fears are, we can by knowing them let them go. Fearlessness is simply the honest understanding of our own mortality. Losing our fear is what is important not losing our fear of fighting. A martial artist who has no fear will have no fear of humiliation or defeat.

Not that they are so aggressive and fearsome that nobody will challenge them, not because they are able to knock people around but because they are open hearted non judging spontaneous human beings. Responding in life as they do in fighting without forcing, going with the flow. It has been my privilege to know a true Master of an art, the art of living.

23

Students & Teachers

In the early 60's I studied at the Taipei Koushu Federation in Taiwan. My teacher Mr. Ch'en Mei Shou was keen to teach his five element Hsing-I, but put us through 3 months of general Koushu forms first. He liked to linger with us over a pot of soup, feathers still on the chicken, and offer some reflections. One evening he shook his head back and forth and said, "*I am really not teaching in the right way! If I was teaching in the right way I would teach the rooting first, but then all the students would run away. First, I have to know your character!*"

Twenty Five years later I was visiting Ben Lo's class at the Clement Street School. That evening was the second session of a new beginning class. It was the middle of the winter and not many students came. Ben turned to me and said, "I have to ease up. I have already eased up. If I teach the way I used to teach, all the students will run away."

A few years later at one of the camps, Ben invited Marshall Ho as a visiting guest Master. Ben Lo and Abraham put on quite a show. Abraham and a student (Bill Helm maybe) did what he called his "A&B" form (san shou), which he apologized for, saying that it was a "smuggled form," not really one derived from Professor Cheng's teachings. Then it was Marshall Ho's turn to perform, but Marshall was relatively new to Tai Chi and he did not have the demonstrable soulful form that Ben and Abraham had demonstrated. He spoke before he demonstrated saying something to this effect: You are all very fortunate to have such great accomplished Masters to study with. Their form shows the highest level of Tai Chi practice. I do not have such fine form to show you. I have not studied so intensely. I only began to learn Tai Chi when I was an older person, but I am teaching many students. "I must say I believe a little bit of Tai Chi is good for everyone."

The Master struggles to make his teaching method and art adaptable to the times that we live in.

Gregg expressed his appreciation for the time that he shared during his recent visit with me and my students. The visit raised questions for him. What do you do once you have made a significant investment in the basics to achieve a higher level of demonstrable skill in the push-hands? We have to consider the teacher-student relationship and also the potential to develop your art with a practice partner of your choice.

There is a big difference between how I relate as a teacher to a student who has only recently gotten a hunch that he or she would like to try a little Tai Chi and a more advanced student. New students may not yet know what Tai Chi is. For a hundred students heading into the form for the first time, maybe one will continue to practice. Then there is the student whose interest in Tai Chi has already matured. He or she has read a good deal of the literature, completed the basic form, and now expresses some enthusiasm about further cultivations. The teacher has to sense that there is mutual respect. The teacher is looking for students whom he or she can teach full heartedly. But when is the right time for some extra work, details and shared insight? How much time do you have? Does your Tai Chi interest-maturity permit you to recognize the opportunity that a teacher offers you? What kind of opportunity are you looking for?

Teaching is not just about more basics. Teaching is about *special knowledge*. Where do you get this special knowledge? I am thinking about your concerns, Gregg, and I suspect this is what you are inquiring about. Tai Chi is an art. Each artist has his own taste. We choose from the elements which come to our attention in this great debate and in our personal experience. Push-hands leaves plenty of room for impulse, eccentric timing and creative solutions. Some recognize classical lessons in a personal way that make those specific lessons their basics by choice. "...the spirit rising from the bottom of the spine--which is kept ram-rod straight and in a plumb erect position ...," for example.

That form correction does in fact carry over into the push-hands is basic, foolish to argue with fundamentally, but subject to myriad interpretations. The feeling of buoyancy, the possibility of tilting the pelvis, a momentary rise or fall, is also part of the push-hands art. How do you weigh each stated principle relative to another? When is one idea more urgent than another? When must you stick to your root dead-nuts on--this is all part of the special knowledge that you go about collecting. Having stored experience in silence over many years a teacher may then be able to articulate points that have become cognitive to him or her, maybe not. But you have to be able to feel what the teacher is doing. You have to have access to higher level practice. There has to be a spirit to spirit investment, teacher to student, student to teacher, student to student. This takes a significant investment in time and it is a learning path that can not be embarked upon without matured interest and mutual respect.

Students come and visit my classes in Seattle from time to time. They have come from cities in China, from Taipei--ah but mostly from California! From the perspective that I have as a teacher I can tell you that I always feel that I never get enough one on one time with any one. People are way too committed and busy when they travel to visit classes. Modern life.

Take a look at this response that I received yesterday from an old student who I invited for some extra practice in the park during his proposed visit to Seattle:

"I don't know if your suggestion was for you and me and perhaps Pam or if you might still lead practice if there were six of us. Tim, Pam's oldest, lives in Seattle, and has the baby for Saturday. Mary Wong is full Chinese, lives in Seattle and met Pam on the internet, then subsequently met Tim. All expressed interest. Lotta options. Anything goes. I'll be in touch." A second email arrived a day later altering the plans to invite me to dinner instead. The times given were exactly the times that I told them in advance that I had a regular scheduled Tai Chi class which de facto they have already talked themselves out of. I get used to it. I certainly am not going to miss my class!

There is some old Chinese etiquette advice: "Don't leave the dinner table until after the older guests leave." Now I am surely becoming one of the older guests and I am feeling that the younger guests are leaving too soon. When I first heard Martial Ho's remark that a little bit of Tai Chi is good for every one, knowing our seriousness at the time, I protested. Now I can think of many people who would be better off with just that little bit. I have to sincerely ask myself if I am teaching in the right way. We each have few hours in which to choose our priorities. No blame. I can tell you though, that there are several students that I would really like to spend much more time with, but they have a million things to do.

My interest in the Push-hands is in either winning with ease, comfort and relatively soft light knowledgeable application, or when trapped, losing easily. I think panting and getting all worked up during push hands, trying to win every point, demonstrates nothing more than one's own ineptness.

This is the view that I hold dear. Someone else may have a different way of stating their personal goals.

I don't care for ritualized demonstrations. I need to enrich the basics and then move on to the special knowledge. I never play the role of dummy stand-in for a stunt man demo. I never ask my students to take a posture ready to be defeated. I will give hours of toe to toe push-hands exposure to anyone who is mature enough and interested enough. Hopefully we will sit down together for an hour or so I can have a reasonable humane exchange with an interested student.

Were I to choose a teacher at this stage of my development, he or she would have to be the kind of person who would invite me stand in for an hour or so of push-hands. Otherwise I will arrange to meet a practice partner and we will get in a juicy two hour session. I don't need a teacher to tell me to just practice more basics.

(By analogy) from the Yellow Emperor's Ling Shu:

"For every needling, the method is above all not to miss the rooting in the Spirits."

Some sort of metaphysics is involved.

Special knowledge in Tai Chi and in push-hands will not come easily.

24

Tai Chi and Cognitive Therapy

This is written by someone who has recently suffered from official stress and tension (not just the "Oh, I'm stressed today," version but the real thing), and related mild depression. I decided that getting to the bottom of the thinking aspects was the only way to get out of the terrible, "I can't cope," state you get into in these situations. Mild medication was prescribed but you still have that deep internal screaming that says, "But I don't know how to," when people say, "Just take it easy, and relax". I sought the help of a qualified psychologist.

I learned that we internalise things; these things build up, our bodies can only take so much – until with this stress addition the stress "jug" overflows. At this stage getting the jug below full is impossible. The simplest daily thing will throw you back over the top again.

Fight or Flight

If you are *actually* threatened by a wild animal, by someone attacking you, by any such physical thing then the brain tells the body to release extra adrenalin for Fight or Flight.

Also, if you *feel* threatened by non-physical things (a bad meeting, an interview, a worrying letter, etc) then your brain similarly stimulates the adrenalin – as the brain cannot distinguish between the different types of threat. However, in these situations you can't generally fight or "run" – there is no where to "go". You get on a continual adrenalin "high" where everything seems a threat, the adrenalin causes your muscles to overwork and tense, you get fidgety, you get annoyed, you are continually using energy – with no rest time to rebuild your energy levels. The "flight" manifests itself as avoidance – you avoid meeting people, going out, doing mundane tasks – you *have to* keep to your comfort zone (which is often your bed).

Adrenalin is a very powerful "drug" coupled with a very powerful brain, the effects of which can have a dramatic effect on your body and how you react to threats. Your confidence goes, you continually think negative thoughts. Basically, you lose the ability to function correctly – you lose control.

So perhaps you're thinking, "He's now going to say I started doing Tai Chi and all got better". No sorry. I was so tired that even doing Tai Chi exercises was not possible – it was that bad!

The Meeting of the Ways

So what is he trying to tell us. Well, it is what I see as the very close relationship I found between the basic concepts of Tai Chi and those of Cognitive Therapy. Cognitive Therapy is targeted at relaxing your mind and body (and thinking differently about the various forms of negative thinking). To not anticipate the future, to not look back at the bad times, and to live for this second.

So if we can avoid *feeling* threatened by an opponent – even the very subtle attack/movement of an opponent in push hands – then we can avoid even the slightest adrenalin rush, we remain relaxed, and we can remain in control and can calmly deal with the situation.

You must always have a relaxed mind, not just your body. You must learn to take things in your stride and relax through even that tiny feeling of annoyance/adrenalin you get when someone does something you disagree with, argues with you, etc! Remember the statement in Tai Chi which says, "Every atom of your body must always be relaxed".

Then **there is no opponent, there is no attack**.

Relax, Relax, Relax – Mind and Body

The key learning points for me from Cognitive Therapy are as follows:

1. Slow down (wait, absorb, and slowly proceed).

2. Do not anticipate.

3. Live in this second.

To me these match exactly the very basic and the most fundamental of teachings of Tai Chi, if not fully implemented then other aspects of Tai Chi become impossible, and captured in the statement, "**The qi is everywhere** in the body, without the slightest obstruction".

Stress, anxiety and tension are real. They are born from the natural human instinct of Fight or Flight – so be prepared – **aim to always have a relaxed mind and body**.

(Please note – the writer is not a qualified psychologist but has written this based on personal recent experiences only).

"Wisely and slow, they stumble that run fast" – William Shakespeare

Slow down, and wait …

A drunken man who falls out of a cart, though he may suffer, does not die. His bones are the same as other people's, but he meets his accident in a different way. His spirit is in a condition of security. He is not conscious of riding in the cart; neither is he concious of falling out of it. Ideas of life, death, fear and the like cannot penetrate his breast; and so he does not suffer from contact with objective existence. If such security is to be got from wine, how much more is to be got from God?

Chuang-tzu

25

Rose Coloured Glasses (or how to unwrap a brick!)

Writing about the art has never been a problem for me in the past, but because of certain instances and attitudes I have discovered in the world of Tai Chi Chuan, I felt the need to step back and reassess my own feelings and try to understand the people I have encountered. I have had to acknowledge that even Tai Chi cannot escape the internal problems of all Martial Arts i.e. *the wrong people in the wrong art at the wrong time for the wrong reasons*. The following article may reflect some of my disappointments, but also my hopes for the road ahead, and the need for us all to sometimes be still, and reflect before moving on again

Before someone trod on my rose coloured glasses, I had a long honeymoon with Tai Chi. Like most beginners my husband and I looked with awe and admiration at our teacher and his masters. We were inspired by their dedication and skill, and felt that they opened many closed doors of ignorance to a better understanding of what the art held in store for us, if we worked hard and had the desire to want more than the average night school class could provide.

I thank them for implanting that vision, but I now realise, some years on, although their exterior packaging was excellent, *however you wrap a brick it is still a brick!* This is one of my favourite sayings as I write. It's understandable that when we first commence training, in anything, we are susceptible to this outward appearance of worth, otherwise we would not start at all. We value our instructor's expertise and hopefully he or she has a reputation as a good and reliable person.

If I say that when we formed our club **Kai Ming** (open-minded), the other choice of title was *Beware the Brick*; need I say more. If we could have translated it into Chinese there would have been no contest for the title. Tai Chi seems to have within the art, many pedestals, with "Masters" teetering on them, elevated there, by various avenues. Possibly the main misleading factor is the mystical propaganda surrounding it. We have come to believe that anyone involved for a long period of time will have a definite understanding of the essence, plus the "Good heart" of the Taoist and will guide us with skill and humility, in the hope that one day we can attain their level, and in time pass it on to the next generation. Forget it! Unfortunately this does not apply to some. The general rule appears to be, if they started out on the Tai Chi journey, as an arrogant self-worshipping waster, you can bet your life they still are. The art can do many things for you, but a personality transplant is not one of them! To the average student who may only stay for a while, this person may do no lasting damage, but if, as we did, you want a lifelong relationship with the art, it would be devastating to one day "unwrap the brick".

Fortunately I now realise that these people are eventually of no consequence. You hopefully find them out, and move on. Thankfully there are Masters I have met, who by their sheer goodness, inside and out, have made me feel humble in their presence. The one who springs to mind at times of disillusionment, and there have been many, was a Master whom I met, on the occasion of his first trip away from Malaysia where he was born. He trained every day for hours in the early morning when it was cool, and again in the evening after work, before retiring around 9 pm, to rise at 5 am to begin again. Above his bed was an iron bar to reach up and grasp, as a conditioning aid for extra training. In the daytime he had a heavy metal bowling ball on a stand, which he picked up and put down constantly when not busy, even his feet where not idle, as he had a device to exercise them whilst sitting!

He did not hold open classes, and had only one private student. He had no desire to become revered by others, he trained for himself, and the benefits he believed he could obtain from his art. Then the news came that his elderly teacher had died, and as former disciples met each other again after the funeral, he was deeply worried when he heard them discussing how much of their master's teachings they had forgotten. It was at this moment that he realised he could remember it all. He also knew then that if he did not pass it on, it could be lost forever. He came thousands of miles to England leaving his village for the first time, because of his love and belief in his art. His name was Master Liang He Ching of Malaysia (5th May 1936 – 1st July 2007).

The other side of the coin is the Master who although has many skills and has trained with many teachers, sells his art at greatly inflated prices, keeping the best for him, and using the money to avert the need for a "real job". Neither my husband nor any of the instructors in our club teach for a living, because to do this and support a mortgage it is inevitable that you have to "prostitute" yourself to a certain degree, by the need to obtain sufficient funds. Suffice to say the only one of our instructors who told me at the onset of his training that he could see a good living to be made, once he had obtained his grade, has been voted out of our association because of his bad attitude and other deeds. He is now teaching for a club where some of the members are like minded. What is to be said about Wasters?

I suppose it's being too idealistic to have expected Tai Chi to escape the politics that other martial arts attract; the secret is not to get caught up in them, and allow it to detract from the pleasures you are obtaining in training, something that I have not always found easy. Teachers who have no confidence in their skills or worse, those who have too much, would eventually be found out one hopes. I once heard it said that *Great Masters go unnoticed* which can be translated to mean that they have no need to be flash, no need to prove anything to themselves or anyone else. It saddens me how people are so easily misled, and this does not only apply to newcomers to the art. One of our students who had trained with us for some years, but due to work commitments had to leave, eventually found another class nearer his home, which had not long ago been set up. When my husband saw him a few months later and asked how he was getting on, he was told he hadn't been able to "sit in" until he had made a commitment by paying £100 term fee, and added that some of the exercises he had been show made his knees hurt. These exercises where in contradiction to those a teacher had taught him in our club, a club recognised by the governing bodies for Tai Chi Chuan. When we suggested that he should know good from bad by now, he amused us by saying his Sifu must know what he is doing "because he is Chinese". How long must this cultural blindness go on? If my son went to China would he be regarded as a Cricket Master, just because he played a little in his youth There are well known cases in England, one where a guy who worked in a Chinese restaurant spotted an opening in the Tai Chi market, and developed his own system, which should be known as Infinite Rubbish although he did initially claim it was a "Family System". Maybe I should be an authority on Faggots and Peas as I live quite near to the "Black Country" where they are a choice dish.

Whenever we begin new classes, we have found it to be good policy to invite prospective students to a free demonstration class. They can see what they will be getting or at least the potential of what they can hope to achieve. Questions can be asked, credentials checked, misconceptions cleared and medical problems discussed. Those who are unsure will now be able to make an informed decision, and others will have saved themselves money by attending.

Whenever we begin new classes,
we have found it to be a good policy ...

26

Trying to avoid my destiny ...

We are led, aren't we? Even if we are at the time unaware.

Little did I realise when my husband finally found a fairly local Tai Chi class, that my life was about to change. Not a miraculous transformation. Not immediate enlightenment. But a slow dawning.

My usual defensive excuses about my arthritic knee joints and 'bad back' weren't accepted and I was persuaded to "come along and try for myself". I don't mind telling you it was almost impossible to coax seized up knees to just gently and lightly bounce. But I was made to feel relaxed enough and welcome enough to only do as much as was comfortable – which I have to say was very little to begin with. Since when has exercise been this easy? No goals. No time limits. No competition. Even better, no jarring of joints, no stress and *no pain*.

I had always thought it was 'no pain, no gain'. Wrong. With Tai Chi I found it was no pain, everything to gain. I began to see that Tai Chi's gentle movements strengthened my leg muscles, taking the strain off my knee joints, therefore allowing greater mobility and flexibility. It also promotes correct posture which removed any strain from my lower back. I have recently been encouraged to hear my osteopath recommending Tai Chi.

I Hope Nobody's Watching !

Perhaps at this point I ought to say how I really felt when my husband and I first joined. Embarrassed – comes to mind. Not so much because I didn't achieve a great deal in the first few weeks, but more so the fact that our teacher was so genuinely enthusiastic about a series of movements which

quite frankly looked ridiculous. They seemed to be so easy and I couldn't imagine how they were going to 'exercise' my body. I was relieved to be in an enclosed hall with no onlookers. How on earth were these small movements going to be of benefit to me? I'd always seen keep-fit enthusiasts putting so much effort into their chosen sporting pursuits and now faced with a young man effortlessly drifting around the room spouting about the health giving properties of Tai Chi, I was hard pushed not to laugh.

I think an apology is long overdue.

Little did I know that I had been led to an all encompassing holistic art form which has, over the years, gently revealed itself to me to be not just an aerobic, no-impact relaxing discipline, but also a means of balancing the body's physical and mental energies and of becoming a spiritually uplifting even prayerful experience.

Tai Chi Practitioners Do It In The Park!

If I can overcome my self consciousness and join Alan in the park, Tai Chi in the morning or evening underneath the old trees is very rejuvenating. Amusing also when we are joined by the occasional teenager who is determined to try out his very vocal Bruce Lee impersonation. There have been times when we've lost track of time and been locked in the park at dusk. I can just imagine the local headlines!

We're All Individuals

We're all unique, and as such come to Tai Chi with our own unique reasons and expectations. Some come because it is a Martial Art, others seek relaxation and some like me, hoping to find a gentle form of exercise. But just as we are taught that if you have joined a class for relaxation you will also learn the martial aspects and improve your body's efficiency, and similarly if you have come solely for the martial training you may be surprised to find you're learning how to relax and improve your health as a bonus – I definitely found far more than I ever expected.

Yes my knees are so much better that people disbelieve that I ever had a problem with them. But there's so much more I don't know where to start. It was a while before I realised that Tai Chi had improved my circulatory system and I no longer suffered leg cramps during the night – something I'd inherited from both parents and experienced since childhood. I now stand naturally with my knees directly above my feet as opposed to being slightly knock-kneed, again an inherited problem which must be why my family are predisposed to arthritic knees. Linked with this are dropped arches which I now find have disappeared because I automatically bear my weight correctly. My driving is far more laid-back as find I have a calmer and more forgiving nature, not bad for someone renowned for her quick temper. I find half an hour of Tai Chi calms the mind, energises the body and lifts the spirits. Perfect at the end of a stressful day.

I have to come clean and admit that on more than one occasion my commitment has wavered. Twice following surgery and also after the death of my very closest friend, Len, I stayed away from classes for many months at a time, but somehow I knew it was o.k. to begin again. And yes, each time I stopped my knees seized up again and the leg cramps returned. But it's comforting to know that you won't be judged, just welcomed back to class and allowed the space and time to develop.

27

How to be a Tree – the Root of the Problem

Over the last twelve months I have on three occasions been within a hair's breadth of falling over, and most probably injuring myself. Once when I slipped backwards on wet leaves as I left work, once when I tripped up on a curb when walking my dogs, and the third time when a young child stopped dead directly in front of me as I as walking forward at quite a pace. By adjusting my centre of gravity and regaining my root (connection to the earth) I was able to avoid the humiliation of falling flat on my back or face as the case may be.

At the critical moment, just as I was about to reach the point of no return, my brain automatically took over and set into motion all the body mechanics I had learnt in my years of practicing Tai Chi and the day was saved (or should I say my face).

It was purely an automatic action, which I have evolved because of my practice of the form and perhaps even more importantly, developing my root, my connection with the ground beneath my feet, keeping my spine aligned (as if suspended from above) – after all if you are suspended how can you fall over? All of these things apply when pushing hands, being pushed over after all is caused by the same principles as losing your balance and falling over – no root and poor body alignment leading to poor balance.

As students progress in their training they commence their search for 'the golden root'. It's no wonder they look bemused when they are told that when pushed whilst practicing, to let the force go into their root. And where, if they dare ask, is this root? "Simple, in the ground like a tree," replies the instructor. How you get it there is the difficult bit.

Roots are funny things, they are not visible to the naked eye, you cannot simply purchase them, and frequently just when you think you have at last got one, oops, someone half your size pushes you over whilst playfully pushing hands in class. You try to push them back, but lo and behold discover they seem to have a root on par with an oil drill.

You may feel that if you are not interested in cultivating the martial aspects of Tai Chi Chuan then you do not need a root; maybe you can take a short cut to form excellence with one less skill to develop. Wrong. Unfortunately there is no way to go except all the way. Every principle that has been developed along the Tai Chi path is necessary, and personally I think rooting is one of the fundamental skills to focus on even at the beginning of your training. You will hear your teacher incessantly saying "Sink into your root, know where you are placing your feet, be aware of your connection to the ground, receive the force and mentally direct it down through your body through the point in your foot and into the earth". Remember the saying, "Where the mind goes the Chi goes". I know this to be true because as soon as I started concentrating on emptying and filling my legs (with each weight change) when practicing the form, my legs began aching. My mind was definitely there, so was my chi by the feel of it, in abundance! Try it sometime.

The mind is a powerful thing as we all know. Just think of the fakirs who lie on beds of six nails and then have people stand on them. Because they believe they will not be harmed nor the skin pierced, they relax and nothing happens to them. So on that basis if you believe as I do that a tree with a deep root cannot be moved and your 'roots' are firmly embedded in the ground, then who can move you? You must however remember, even though you are firmly rooted your body must remain relaxed and flexible, your branches able to 'bend with the wind' or perhaps more appropriately deflect a blow.

It is said the Chinese believe we die from the feet upwards (which I interpret as becoming immobile); so if you keep your legs strong you'll live a long healthy life. Tai Chi will certainly give you strong legs, it will increase your muscle power thereby removing the strain from your joints and in turn making them last longer. However none of these wondrous benefits will occur without hard work, mentally and physically; Tai Chi may look effortless to the casual observer, but I have learned to beware of the effortless punches. Like many things, the best results come when you are not really trying that hard, and really that is what the art is all about; let your body move freely, don't resist, be grounded, firm but relaxed and perfectly balanced.

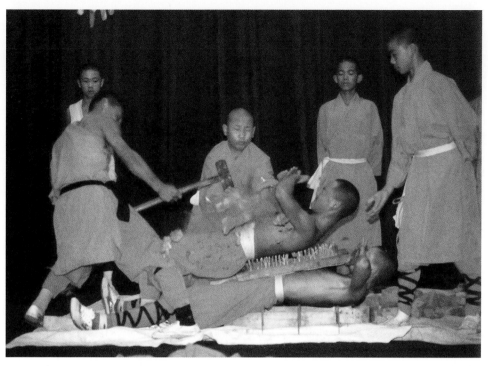

Chinese Wushu experts demonstrating extraordinary techniques

Always remember the tree: the trunk and roots are still and strong, the branches when young are strong but yielding. If we keep ourselves supple, practicing our Tai Chi, hopefully we will remain supple well into old age. Perhaps we cannot change our genes, but at least we can give them all the help we can.

Patience is quiet hope and trust that things will turn out right. You wait without complaining. You are tolerant and accepting of difficulties and mistakes.

Patience is a commitment to the future.

This character contains the ideas for both patience, perseverance and endurance. This single character can be a bit ambiguous or flexible as it can also mean to endure, to bear, to put up with.

28

Connections

In all honesty Tai Chi is an art form that I would never have considered as part of my lifestyle. Perhaps, after being influenced as a child by the traditional martial arts movies, I had tried Judo and Karate as a young man. I enjoyed Judo but found Karate focused too much on aggression. Anyway as a nurse my shift pattern did not allow regular exercise of any kind. Long hours of work, study and lifting heavy patients took its toll. However I enjoyed the work and after qualifying as an Adult Nurse I went on to qualify both in Children's Nursing and Midwifery. Externally I served as an Officer in the reserve forces and enjoyed a wide variety of adventure training including parachuting, sailing, and similar activities.

However, as the years went on I started to suffer from the traditional nurse's occupational illness – the dreaded bad back. I had injured myself as a student and progressively it got worse. It began to affect the things I did outside work. I had two unsuccessful epidurals and modified the type of work I did in order to avoid heavy lifting. I gave up delivering babies and went to work in a children's hospice.

I got married in 1994 and my wife invited a friend to the wedding. Her husband turned out to be the senior instructor of the Kai Ming Tai Chi club. He suggested taking up the discipline but it was to be another five years before I started to learn the form and the breathing exercises associated with Tai Chi.

Working in a hospice is often a difficult task when you know that the children you are working with have not been given the advantages in life that most of us have. However the hospice tries to be a happy place and benefits from beautiful landscaped gardens. Although stressful at times, working in the area is a great privilege and I have learned two important lessons in life from the children. Firstly have no regrets. Follow whatever dreams you have, even if they don't work out. At least you will know you have tried. Secondly try and do something each day that reminds you that you are alive and not just someone stuck in the rat race going through the motions.

That is how I started to take up Tai Chi. I am far from being an expert. Shift work is still a problem and it has taken me a very long time to learn what I have. I can't attend classes on a regular basis as I also have to study but I have been fortunate that my instructor takes time to help me out with a little personal tuition.

The result has been I have not had a back pain related sick day in two years. It is not a problem any more. Frankly being trained in the art of western medical science I am at a loss to explain it. However, more important than that I enjoy the form. I have practiced in the rain, a snowstorm and once during thunder and lightning. Perhaps that is a bit extreme but on a normal day in the garden I notice birds and plants and hear sounds that would usually be in the background un-noticed. Last month I parachuted for the first time in seven years. Its nice to be alive!

29

Tai Chi Chuan Principles over Techniques

There is no real excellence in this world
which can be separated from right living.

David Starr Jordan

I have been meaning to write this for a long time, but never seemed to get started. I think it was a combination of Jenny Peters nagging me and recently reading a book by Stephen Covey called *The Seven Habits Of Highly Effective People*. I expect you have realised from the title that this isn't a book about martial arts at all, but one of a myriad of 'power management' books that seem to endlessly flood the market. I borrowed this book from my managing director initially in an attempt to find out what made him tick (he's got shelves full of this stuff) but after dipping into a few pages, I soon realised it put in words what Tai Chi Chuan aims to put into action.

Whether people come to Tai Chi for health and relaxation or to learn a self defence they invariably want a series of quick fix techniques for a fast result. Although techniques are easily learned, they are just as easily forgotten. To be effective in the long term they have to become natural and instinctive, but by their sheer nature techniques are static; it is the underlying principles which give them life. Virtually everybody knows to bend your knees not your back when lifting a heavy package, and we all say it makes common sense. This is not just a technique but a *principle* of proper body mechanics. Where Tai Chi differs from external muscular based martial arts is not just due to its focus on the mystical energy called *chi* but due to its awareness of the principles of proper body mechanics. A large proportion of those first attending Tai Chi are suffering from stress, poor circulation, joint damage, cardio-vascular problems etc. The art has become renowned for its health giving qualities more so than its martial prowess; why is this? It is because of its core focus on correct body function. The principles that underlie Tai Chi Chuan are the principles by which our mental and physical systems are designed to operate efficiently. That which is natural happens without effort, that which is forced has its limitations.

Through correct body alignment strain is taken from the joints and the load is placed in the muscles and tendons, providing the function they were designed for. The knee is one of the most frequently damaged joints, whether by martial training or bad luck, but this one joint is supported by a series of muscles and tendons that are designed to articulate it and absorb any shock. Use this joint correctly and it will give you a lifetime of trouble free use; abuse it by not adhering to the principles of proper function and see what happens. The Tai Chi classics are like a rule book for proper body function. Follow their principles closely and you will not only stave off injury but improve the body's efficiency. One principle Professor Man Ch'ing put great store in was "Make your spine upright". Apart from the effect it has on your skeletal structure and organ alignment, it also aids the effect of 'rotating like a wheel', with your spine aiding the creation of an axis. This is explored in great depth in *Cheng Tzu's 13 Treatises on Tai Chi Chuan*. My intention here is only to reinforce the need for proper body alignment and function, as we have covered this issue before, so keep this in the back of your mind when we consider the importance of *principle over technique*.

Jan Diepersloot said, "External martial arts are based on the energy of movement, whereas internal martial arts are based on the movement of energy. We can consider this in terms of the effort taken (both mental and physical) to apply techniques compared to free flow when applying correct principles. I am constantly asked by students for applications for Tai Chi Chuan forms; these are usually ex-students of external arts who are used to drilling applications. Here comes the difficulty; learning applications to the form helps you have an intent when practising, helps you remember the postures, allows you to check body alignment and so on; what they are not is wholly practical. The core concept is 'from Wuji to Taiji' or more clearly, from non-action to action. This means that an input is required to create a reaction thereby making Tai Chi a defensive (or better still reactive) art rather than an offensive one (unless of course you swear at your attacker as well!). Reacting doesn't allow for time delay while deciding which technique to choose nor does it

allow time to switch to a backup if the first fails. Unfortunately techniques are quicker to learn and seemingly easier to grasp than principles; how do you convince a student that it is better to blend with an attack than to block it, to allow the body to 'stand like a balance and rotate like a wheel' thereby receiving and redirecting the energy instead of just smashing it out of the way. This is what Professor Cheng called *'Investing in loss'*.

Self-defence is not just about physical attack, it is about mental attack as well; the stresses and strains of everyday life: traffic queues, over-bearing bosses, missing Coronation Street, being late for *my* class. In terms of personal interaction, referring back to Covey, he named these two areas *personality and character ethic*. He stated that character ethics included integrity, humility, patience, simplicity and modesty which were the basic principles for effective living, whereas personality ethics included public image, skills and techniques designed to lubricate the process of human interaction i.e. being manipulative and even deceptive. He believed that our character ethics are in our nature and only need to be nurtured whereas personality ethics are only superficial tricks to gain a 'quick fix' and would soon fail or be found out. We have all at sometime or other seen both ethics in action but it has only been more recently that I have considered them in terms of martial development. Principles for proper living and principles for effective fighting are invariably the same; they are non-confrontational and follow the *Tao*.

Techniques covering locking, throwing and striking are taught to understand their function but they are limited by *what ifs*. To properly apply any methods, the underlying principles are what makes them *real*. People don't attack in the same way with a nice clean straight punch or a grab to your right wrist. Sitting loosely into your hips so that the body feels buoyant and allowing the waist to move freely, strictly adheres to the principles of this wondrous art. An input of energy will cause a natural reaction in the Tai-Chi'I practitioner, subduing or throwing out the attacker.

No techniques are considered, only the principles of adhering, redirecting and releasing. As soon as a forced technique is applied, the attacker has something to resist thereby giving them an opportunity to counter. Principles are simple and therefore know no bounds; techniques are just that, and limited by their nature. When students ask what would you do if I hit you, I have to reply, "I have no idea but it is likely to hurt". Apart from the obvious intended discouragement (well I don't really want them to hit me!!), this statement is true because without the energy input of an attack I cannot move from *Wuji* to *taiji*.

Consider the principle of *borrowing your opponent's strength*. If we look at the body as a see-saw in balance (Zhong Ding) and the fulcrum as our centre (Dan Tien) then an input to one side (a strike) will cause an equal and opposite output (counter-attack) on the other side. A technique would be a strike and counter whereas the function of the see-saw allows this principle to be used against any input and more importantly, the greater the input the greater the output; *this is the only martial art where attackers beat themselves up!!* Another example which may be clearer to other martial artists is *the intercepting fist*. This is applied by punching across the attacker's striking arm, directly at their centre; it intercepts their strike rather than blocking it and allows you strike to land. The technique is called *intercepting fist* but the underlying principle allows you to strike, break the limb, throw etc. If too much force is used the attacker will have a chance to counter; using Professor Cheng's theory of *'never put more than four ounces on them and never let them put more than four ounces on you'*, (as an extension of *deflect 1000 pounds with four ounces*) allows you to move your body to a better position if the attacker's strike is too powerful. The shortest distance between two points is not always the straightest; technique alone does not allow for this.

Tai Chi Chuan is famous for *rooting* but how does it work? There are many pictures of great masters absorbing a push from a whole bunch of people at once; this is not done by just wedging themselves between the pushers and the floor because if the pushers moved, the master would fall over. The principle of *seek the straight within the curve* allows the force to be directed to the ground through a seemingly straight line, while the curve generated by soft (buoyant) joints allows the master to absorb and release at will. Rooting is a feeling of connection to the ground, through the whole body, and can be just as easily felt when sitting *wei tso* (with upright spine), standing on tip toe or moving around. The principle of *go backwards to go forwards, go down to go up* etc. allow you to sever your opponent's root or rather their feeling of stable connection to the ground; the effortless throws of Aikido work in the same way. Rooting allows you to use the strength of the ground to defend and attack in the same instant; simply put, if you punch an opponent with a feeling of connection from the ground to your hand, the ground can not move therefore the opponent will. I always tell people the key to self-defence is to *take your opponent's balance while maintaining your own*; balance is both mental and physical therefore by feeling rooted, balanced and calm you will eventually be able to deal with all the stresses of life and see them coming a mile away. In terms of physical attack, you can move as necessary, counter (effect their physical balance) and disorientate them putting them at the disadvantage (affect their mental balance).

I hope I haven't waffled on too much in my attempt to get the point across. The best way forward is patience and a good teacher (or just pay me).

30

Close Encounters of the Strange Kind

Call me a sceptic, but as soon as someone says to me "I can feel your Chi", or, "I think I have too much Yin and not enough Yang" I'm out of there!

Once a student actually told my husband he could see an aura of light around him, and was sure that if he got too close, he would be thrown backwards by the power it contained. Well, all that told *me* was that perhaps my husband should have put on more deodourant that day! I'm not saying he doesn't have his attractions, and I must admit I was bowled over when I first met him, but I can assure you also that it had nothing to do with his Tai Chi talents, good as they may be!

You can read many, many articles on the art's mystical attributes, and that's fine, but when our association, Kai Ming, was formed, the committee of instructors decided our prime purpose was to open up the enigma that is Tai Chi, demystify it, look for western terms that could explain the eastern ones more clearly, and help people realise there is no magic. The Masters are only ordinary mortals who wanted that little bit more, so trained a great deal more.

I believe the true magic is within us all. The human body is the greatest tool we own. It has incredible engineering, wondrous powers of self healing, an efficient heating system (with built in thermostat), and ingenious plumbing linked to the waste disposal unit. Its electrical circuits alone would leave our computers standing. So why do most of us pay out lots of money for contracts to maintain these systems in our houses, but mostly leave our best investment, our bodies, to look after themselves ?

I'm a nurse, and I think Tai Chi may be the key to the apprenticeship of maintenance which we need. Also, maybe because I'm a nurse, I cannot equate with chi and meridians, for these I substitute oxygen and circulation, now those I can understand.

I have just read two articles written by people who feel they have experienced life-changing benefits from the art. This is wonderful. It is great that this has happened, and that they have felt elated enough to tell the world, the only problem I personally have with this is that both of them only acknowledged the yin or soft female qualities of Tai Chi, which is in itself, talking unbalance! Yin and Yang, Male and Female, Hard and Soft, Light and Dark, they all go together.

The one chap repeatedly said we should use Tai Chi in everyday life, when working, driving, shopping, socializing, sleeping. But although I waited patiently throughout the whole epistle, he never actually divulged the secret of how to do this. The closest he got was to say you should flow through each day like a river. The theory of this statement is excellent, the instruction on how to attain this ability is sadly lacking!

The second article involved a man "finding himself" in his Tai Chi training, by working through his grief and depression when practicing the form. Obviously there was much more to his story than that, but I began to feel uncomfortable, when in the concluding chapter, he extolled the healing properties of his clothing or hand brushing against parts of his body and the feelings this gave him of washing away his emotional problems by their loving touch. Neither of these men mentioned the whole that is Tai Chi..

As I have said many times before, if you get what you want from the art, and you feel better for it, that's fine, but there is so much more. People should not be misled by only reading this kind of literature that tells you how you should feel instead of advising it is all there, but we may all experience it differently.

We need a balance. There are a vast number of books available on the subject. The popular adage of "the more the merrier" in this art should read, "the more I see the more confused I get". It is extremely difficult for the average student to know good from bad, right from wrong, "pukka from dodgy".

Just try and imagine if you went into a superstore to buy a tin of dog food and discovered they had a whole floor devoted to just that, hundreds and hundreds of the same product, but with a different taste or manufacturer, all professing to be the healthiest, tastiest, and all the same price, how would you decide which to buy, *No, there are none on special offer*. I myself would ask someone who worked there which was the most popular, and in their experience the best. In the case of Tai Chi this would equate with asking your instructor, who has by the time he attains this position, had the unenviable task of sorting the wheat from the chaff. If you follow his advice on what to purchase, you will no doubt find out where he got all those "little pearls of wisdom" from, which you admire him for so much when he quotes them in class supposedly off the top of his head.

Perhaps the main point is, don't believe everything. Just because it's been published doesn't mean it's Gospel. Even as you are reading this, you should be thinking that she may be right, she may be wrong, I'll have a look on her club's website, and see what their view in general is, or email them regarding my own personal interest in the art.

I realise there is a vast market for relaxation and many supposed teachers just teach these techniques. This is in the most part because their own knowledge is limited. These classes should not be advertised as Tai Chi, but as Chinese exercises, or he should say in his literature, "I am going to show you how to make a steak and kidney pie, but I haven't got any kidney to put in it, and I don't know where to get it from. So if you don't know what it tastes like already, you certainly won't by the end of my course, and I'll still charge you full price".

My husband Mark Peters, Principal Instructor for Kai Ming, once attended an introduction night held by one of these supposed teachers, when he was himself looking to begin training, the instructor was quite well known in our city. He came home looking bemused, and told me that the would be students, bearing in mind they were complete strangers, had, after the initial "sales talk", spent several minutes running their hands up and down each others bodies trying to feel the chi! He didn't stay to find out if anyone could feel his.

When he was qualified in the art, before the club was established, and he had other instructors to train with in push hands, he attempted to find teachers from other schools to practice with. Upon telephoning them, one said, "No, I'm afraid you can't come to my class or train with me, but we could sit and talk about Tai Chi if you like." Another who was Chinese said I do not do push hands in my style, his style turned out to be "family style" which in his case meant, after viewing his video, "made up, wave your arms about, look ethereal, twist your knees, hurt your back, no substance style."

So there you have it, after reading about some of our encounters of the strange kind, perhaps you will understand my nervousness when cornered by a *chi* fanatic. I sometimes wish I could develop my own ring of confidence to repel them when overdosed by mystical jargon. When out of interest I looked up the dictionary interpretation of the word mystical it said, "fogginess and unreality of thought, MYSTIFIER – one who or that which mystifies, a hoaxer, MYSTIFY – to make mysterious, obscure, or make secret"

Personally I don't want to be taught by a hoaxer, who's keeping secrets from me, do you? So with this thought I will leave you to ponder the wonders of Real Tai Chi, which I now hope you will be chaffing at the bit to find, whilst I go off polish my aura and balance my Yin and Yang.

FOUR CORNERS

Apply your Tai Chi to the problems of daily life!

31

Tai Chi Chuan Martial Art of Disorientation & Confusion

Think back to when you were a child, When your Mom swung you round and round, set you down and let go of you; remember the feeling you had before you fell over!! Or what about being on a roundabout in the park. Someone would stop it to get on and then perhaps start it going again, but in the opposite direction; remember the giddy disorientated way your head felt, the nausea that rose in your throat and how you staggered when you got off. This is how you hope to make your attacker feel when you use your skills of Tai Chi Chuan properly.

Our bodies are able to remain upright and balanced by a combination of our senses and skeletal structure working together. All muscles and tendons must pull in co-ordination to keep the bones and joints aligned. This however would be of little use if our eyes where shut and we could not focus on our surroundings. Try going down some steps or practising your form/kata with closed eyes. (on second thoughts forget about the steps, we may lose a few students this way!) We all probably know someone who's had dizzy spells (vertigo) because of too much wax in the their ears thus preventing the small fluid filled 'canals' in the inner ear from working properly; this fluid works similarly to a spirit level and helps you to keep your balance. To maintain our balance in our waking hours our brain needs to be able to keep rapid messages reaching various areas to make subtle adjustments. If you are walking or running in one direction and then decide to change, a message is sent informing the receptors in the muscles involved

LOTUS KICK

of your intention to take this action.; the muscles react, the body turns, the eyes adjust their focus and the balance changes – the brain is in control. But what if your direction is suddenly changed, without prior warning to your senses; no adjustment can be made, the messages are scrambled and the brain is confused. When balance is lost, fear and panic abound, as the higher centres struggle to get the body re-aligned. No easy task when you may be flying forward or backwards at a rate of knots. This is what happens when Tai Chi is used in the proper manner against an attack. Look for the weakness in your foe, look for the gaps, his strength will be of no advantage if he is disorientated.

One of the main differences in Tai Chi as a martial art as against external styles is they try to break bones, we try to break the balance whether it be body or mind.

Each time Mark demonstrates applications of any posture, he almost always remarks that the value of them is to help students to remember the actual posture by visualising its martial use. Within the first couple of years practising Tai Chi, I realised that as a martial art it would indeed only work if the true principle were mastered. After six years I suddenly realised that the form and its postures are purely a vehicle to lead us to this extremely difficult state of calmness and relaxation in perhaps the ultimate challenge, the attack that threatens your life, or at least our mental state. Think about it, are you really going to have time as your attacker comes at you with a baseball bat to think to yourself, "Yes, I think a brush-knee twist step would work quite well here", or "If I can just line up my hips, get my feet parallel and scan with my eagle vision, repulse monkey will do quite nicely". *I think not.* Realistically the 'winner' will be the one who can stay calm, use their body as a unit and keep their head when the aggressor is losing theirs. It's got to be your best chance. It's the old adage, 'I am not a victim, I will not be an easy mark' synopsis I have written about before. You always need to face a difficult or frightening situation with a calm mind. When you practice the form, you have to shut out all other thoughts for that time. The breath sinks, the muscles become soft, the mind is focused on the art of relaxation. The blood can flow to all vital organs unobstructed by tension. This is what the cerebral circulation needs, oxygen to keep a clear mind. Without it our thoughts are scattered and illogical, adrenalin and panic will overtake us. How can we not succumb to the dreaded force-meets-force, where the strongest man wins. That is why to be able to use the Tai Chi principles to defend yourself takes a long time, but I am convinced the answer lies in diligent practice of the form. Most of you will have the benefit of discovering this earlier than the six years it took me, because I hope perhaps my words will make you stop and think about the logic of what I'm saying. If you examine your feelings.

To make Tai Chi work for you, it may be that you have to change your perception of yourself and even your attitude. Some people are much better able to handle stressful situations even before they start practising the art. Therefore a naturally placid, relaxed student will probably attain the martial skills earlier than one who has to learn first of all the even harder skills of self control. I defy anyone faced with a threatening situation to initially think, "Well this fellow looks as though he may be going to punch, kick, slap, grab and wrestle me to the floor and jump on my head, but never mind I'm quite calm and relaxed!!". I myself like to believe that the attitude for living when confronted by any problems in life, as offered in Dan Millman's book *Peaceful Warrior* could be used in this situation: feel frightened, feel angry, verbally unwind if necessary and then just let it go, don't hang on to the aggression, it may well be your downfall. This release alone may be enough to make him think twice. If your aggressor still seems intent, then focus on regaining your calm and using his stress against himself. Get back in control, have an advantage.

Recently at a photo-shoot for *Combat*, my husband Mark Peters was constantly hassled by the people in control of the session to look aggressive when demonstrating applications against attacks. He found this very difficult and told them, "But Tai Chi is a martial art with a smile!" In part this may be true, but when I thought about it he has always been a nice non-aggressive person, physically and verbally, since I first met him. Stress has never been a problem, perhaps that is why Tai Chi seemed to come more easily to him than myself, who never fully recovered from the stress of my dad forgetting to collect me from nursery school, until 9 pm, when I was three years old.

I watched a video recently of a children's Karate club, when they were practising sparring with each other in readiness for a competition. My attention became focused on their faces, as they hyped themselves up and went in to strike their opponents. The aggression and violence in their faces was, to me, frightening. It cannot be good for anyone, child or adult, to have to be this hyped up to triumph in confrontation or attack. Harness the available adrenalin, yes, have an intent, yes, but to build yourself up to this degree surely can't be good for the nervous system. I must add these are my own feelings as a parent and nurse, and I'm sure there are many who will disagree, but I do believe in 'everyone to his own', so no letters from Karate instructors please.

I believe that the element which elevates Tai Chi Chuan above other martial arts is it's non-aggressive roots. Surely it is better in a confrontation to diffuse the situation as quickly as possible, using the least violent approach. Better for your opponent to lose their balance, and face, than a few teeth or worse. Very few seek out violence, but if it finds us, we should know the mechanisms that make Tai Chi work. An instructor with our school said to me recently, our association motto should be *"Come and get us if you think you're soft enough!!"* What I gem, wish I'd thought of it.

32

Body Mechanics in Tai Chi Chuan

Believe it or not there is more to Tai Chi than searching for secret points to hit on a Thursday afternoon at 2.30 pm (meridian cycles) or standing in a room full of the misled pretending to be a tree. It is a highly developed and finely tuned system whose underlying foundation is correct body mechanics. To this end a balance of Western and Eastern insight is required. Although applicable to all styles, my background is in Cheng Man Ching style; therefore I will make specific references to his teachings.

Body loading

The compressive loading of the body (due to gravity) is taken through the legs and into the ground (Yongquan point). We use the ankle, knee and hip to form a natural suspension. The weight should fall naturally through the body; here the use of *sung* is implicit. *Sung* is usually translated as relaxation, but may be better described as buoyant relaxation or resilient relaxation; an underlying tenacity is required which is called *Pung* energy. The nearest examples I can think of are trying to push something which is floating down under water and feeling it spring back to its original position; or squeezing a tennis ball and feeling it spring back to its original state. But, if you bend a copper pipe, it stays bent. The difference is the inherent tension. *Sung*, and in turn *Pung*, allows the body to load itself in a buoyant way, without tension, thereby allowing the weight to fall naturally to the floor. The only downside to this is that it really makes your legs ache; when asked, "when will my legs stop aching", Professor Cheng replied, "When you stop improving …"

All of the loosening exercises and standing post (Zhan Zhuang) exercises I was taught are designed to loosen the joints and develop correct body loading; you could say they are the substance of Tai Chi because without them the form is just am empty vessel.

The body can be divided into three section – legs, trunk and arms – each must be correct to release tension and allow correct loading. From the legs is the waist/hip joint (yau-k'ua), which in conjunction with the lower vertebrae, allow free pelvic movement. It says in the Tai Chi classics 'the waist is the commander' and this is the region we are talking about here. Try to imagine this area being similar to the mounting of a ships compass; always seeking a balanced place to rest on a choppy sea, mobility in all directions is essential. In the Cheng system we practice an exercise Mark Hennessy translated as 'constant bear' in his book "Cheng Man Ching: Master of five excellences" (pg. 113). This exercise develops awareness and mobility of the area allowing the coccyx to naturally tuck under, releasing the lower vertebrae and allowing the Wei lu point to fall naturally and the waist to run free; here contractive tension would hinder free movement. The upper body can find its level, without tension, and the weight will fall naturally. With the spine hanging as if suspended from above, by the head-top, each vertebra strung together like a pearl necklace. Now consider the arms; the joints here are the wrist, elbow and shoulder again creating a natural suspension. By raising the hands, dropping the elbows and releasing the shoulders, no unwanted force can be applied and the load will fall naturally through the body. The slightest application of force will trigger a ripple reaction through the body chain, allowing the force to be absorbed and redirected.

Simple rooting exercise – Take up a standard front bow stance (70/30) and place your arms across your chest. Get a partner to push you backwards. As you are pushed into your rear-leg root, focus on trying to release the ankle tendon. This will cause the weight to stay out of the heel and reduce the tendon reflex action. (Professor Cheng stated the last place to relax is the ankle). Next repeat the exercise and grip the floor when pushed; finally let the weight fall through your heel. Note the different feel and effect. Focussing on the tendon will prevent it from causing the leg muscles to contract and therefore allow it to be more suspensive.

Body positioning

Chen Wei-Ming stated that the palms should not extend past the knee (Tai Chi Ta Wen pg.19); this relaxes the chest allowing the breath and chi to sink to the Tan-Tien and reduces the load on the shoulder. Professor Cheng also states that the wrist should naturally extend and be straight in every posture; here this differs from traditional Yang style, which is more extended and bent. By dropping the elbow 'as if a weight was hung from it' the arms can appear almost asleep. Here the angle of the forearm co-insides with the angle of the rear leg (knee to ankle).

Although Cheng stated that the body should be kept upright, this tends to allow people to lean slightly backwards from the waist. As a forward intention is always required, a feeling of slightly leaning forward is more practical; this creates a gentle 'S' shape (gentle curve) through the body, waist and weighted leg. Here the classics state *'Seek the straight within the curve'*. Without this it is virtually impossible to properly load the leg and if a force is applied perpendicular (coming straight into the body horizontally) to your upper body, while your weight is in the front or back leg, the force will be taken in the lower back. A slight 'S' will remove any angles and allow a compressive loading. When the weight is in the front leg the knee must not extend past the toe, and when the weight is in the back leg the bum must not extend past the lower calf/heel. Thereby ensuring the *line of force* from hand to foot is correct (seek the straight within the curve). This compressive loading allows you to receive and release forces similar to bouncing on a trampoline i.e. receive, amplify and release).

The classics state the back should be straight *'as if suspended from above'*; unfortunately a large percentage of people will stand as if suspended from the top of the head rather than the crown (bahui point). The effect of this is to slightly raise the chin, misalign the spine and position the body weight too central i.e. near 50/50. Cheng Man Ching is very clear on the use of 70/30 weighting which requires very specific and subtle body alignment to achieve. By suspending from the crown and *'sinking the chest and plucking the back'*, there is a subtle feeling of leaning forward. I hear you all cry "Wang Tsung-yueh stated, *"don't lean in any direction"* (Lo pg.33), but this statement must be considered in conjunction with other lines in the text, and our understanding of biomechanics. I agree, if you lean in any direction this will break your connection with your waist and disrupt the line of force, but it is the fine line of interpretation that is at play here. Standing too upright can induce an angle at the lower back and break the line of force – again *seek the straight within the curve*.

With the leg joints *soft*, i.e. slightly bent and suspensive at each joint, the weight must fall naturally through the substantial (Yang) leg with the unsubstantial (Yin) leg relaxed but alive. To achieve correct positioning and root the weight should fall through the Yongquan point in the foot, the ankle relaxed, the knee directly above the foot and the hip/waist joint directly above the knee (70/30 front stance); there should also be a connection between the unsubstantial hip/waist joint, knee and foot. This can be explained in terms of the Yin/Yang diagram where there is a little yin in the yang and a little yang in the yin; to be completely yang would be rigid and to be completely yin would be limp. If we look in terms of moments (physics) then to balance the body, where the fulcrum is the weighted leg, the arms and forward intention will counterbalance the empty leg. Although able to momentarily lift the empty leg, the subtle balance means you will be unable to keep it there unless you lean to counterbalance. Examples of counterbalance would be Brush knee twist step (Lou Chi Ao Bu) where the right hand is outstretched in transition, giving balance to the moving left foot, or cloud hands (Yun Shou) where the arms to one side allow the leg at the other to step. Correct use of the rooted fulcrum is essential.

Single weighted postures such as Golden cock stands on one leg (Jing Ji Du Li) or left and right toe kick (Zuo You Fen Jiao) demonstrate balance. To apply power you must be in contact with your attacker and have three legs on the ground, one from you and two from your attacker, creating a tripod. This will release the raised leg to do its damage unimpeded.

Body connection

Motion is rooted in the feet, released through the legs, controlled by the waist and expressed in the fingers. Let the postures be without breaks or holes.

These statements can be read many times but still their subtlety overlooked. The line of force is apparent by the first statement – from the feet to the fingers and back again, whether applied by an attack of just the effect of gravity (generating potential energy). *Without breaks or holes* means to flow continuously by the generation of momentum. Cheng Man-Ching uses the principle of '*Swing and return*' to generate this momentum and in turn apply Kinetic energy. The waist controls the direction and the fingers release the energy. Ben Lo is quoted as saying *Tick Toc* – Tick the attack comes in, Toc the attacker flies out. To be able to receive, direct and release in an instant is the aim of all Tai Chi practitioners.

It is not just what is said, but what remains unsaid that is important. *Waist to the fingers* shows a lack of the need for shoulder or upper body power. When people first push, or even just lift-up their arms, a great deal of shoulder power is used; this is an example of a break in the line of force. When the hand lifts, the elbow and shoulder drops preventing force to land on anything solid (A feather may not be added nor a fly alight). The shoulder blade is set in motion, as is the spine and in turn the hip/waist joint. This motion will continue to flow through the legs, bounce off the ground and back up again. Body connection generates 3D movement in the form of circular motion in all directions. In addition to the above, Cheng also expounds *cross-pumping* i.e. the connection between the opposite hand and foot; sometimes here the posture application is not apparent. With left ward-off (Zuo Peng), it is not the left arm warding off so much as the right hand pulling down that makes the application work; while the left is yielding/neutralising (Yin) the right will break or pull off balance (Yang).

Use Rollback and try feeling as if a piece of string joins your wrist and hip joint together, when you turn feel as if the hip is pulling the wrist. This is a good start on the long road to whole body connection. The classics state here *'When one parts moves all must move'*. To see and feel body connection easily, look to the expansive postures like Single Whip (Dan Bian) and repulse Monkey (Dao Nian Hou). In single whip as the weight transfers into the left leg, the right arm fills and extends (cross-pumping); in repulse monkey as the weight falls into the rear leg, the rear arm draws the force down and the forward arm pushes away, creating a turning wheel effect. Now allow the arms to turn naturally as you perform the movements and start to feel 3D (spiral) motion. This 3D motion is active at every point of the body. Receiving and transmitting energy is done in an instant. *No excess no insufficiency*.

Self-defence

There is more to self-defence than just the ability to overcome an external attacker (mugger, bully, rapist etc). The stresses and strain we put on ourselves everyday far outweigh this likelihood. I tell students' *self-defence is the ability to affect your opponent's physical and mental balance while maintaining your own*. Efficient use of mental and physical effort is at the core of Tai Chi philosophy, to *seek stillness in motion*. Stillness allows you to listen to your body and know if you are making too much effort; try lifting a weight with your arms extended, now lift the same weight closer to your body using your arms and legs. We all know not to bend over when picking something up as it can hurt your back, but there is much more to effective mechanics than that. The statement of *to go, forwards first go backwards* applies not only to uprooting an attacker but also to pushing a heavy wheelbarrow. This action overcomes the initial inertia (root) of an object, once in motion it can be easily accelerated. Koh Ah Teh (Kuala Lumpur, Malaysia) once performed a static push on me as an example of this; his listening skills were so good that he ensured he only applied just enough force to keep me accelerating. When I hit the wall I was shocked at the speed I was moving. Too much force and I would have been able to neutralise, too little and there would have been no effect. By a static push I mean that I inputted no movement to generate the response; I was stood in a 70/30 front stance with my arms crossed across my chest and his hands were lightly touching my forearms.

Applying Tai Chi principles to daily life reduces wear and tear and seemingly increases your abilities; it aids the function or your internal organs improving circulation, digestion and respiration. In fact you are only harnessing your intrinsic ability. Applying the principles in fighting means no force can land on you but you can expel with whole body power at any moment. The biggest fallacy is that Tai Chi is always soft; the ability to balance internal and external is essential to all Chinese Martial Arts. We make constant references to softness and not allowing force to land on you, but little reference is made to delivery other than *like shooting an arrow from a bow* or the use of *whole body power*. I recently read that Cheng Man Ching sometimes felt like concrete when he hit you and I have felt many times the heavy hands of my teacher's (Tan Ching Ngee) strikes. Tai Chi power is like water, searching and unceasing; whether it be the running of a gentle stream or the power of a great tidal wave, what is clear is it is unstoppable …

33

Tai Chi and M.E.

The next time you miss the bus and have to walk home with armfuls of heavy shopping, try to stem the curses for a moment and instead be thankful that you are physically able to do just that!

Most of us today who are blessed with good health take it for granted and punish our bodies in various ways on a daily basis until something happens to make us all too aware of just how precious it is. Then, when we lose it, we turn to our medical profession and demand a quick fix cure to put us back on our feet almost immediately so that we can return to our routine of what amounts to self abuse once more – until something else goes wrong! So it continues until we finally came up against something for which there is no quick fix pill, no ready answer and seemingly no way forward.

In my own case it was M.E. – an illness which I believe is becoming more and more commonplace, affecting people right across the board. There are all sorts of ideas floating about as to what causes it and indeed there are still all too many people who do not acknowledge that it exists at all! I too once thought of it as simply 'yuppie flu' – some sort of malingerers' complaint, the sufferers of which needed a shake and to be told to get their act together – I came to learn the truth in a painfully personal way by falling victim myself to this illness which can be both physically and mentally debilitating to the point where people cam become bedridden for years!

The symptoms can vary from person to person, but usually include disturbance to sleep patterns, heart rhythm abnormalities, painful muscles and joints, fainting, confusion, inability to concentrate, intolerance to bright lights and noise, digestive problems, breathlessness and an overwhelming general fatigue. These stay with you all the time, week after week, month after month, year after year … if you let them.

What many of us do not realise is that we all hold within ourselves vast energies – but we don't know how to tap into them and they often become blocked – I was as much in ignorance of this as anyone and had never taken the time before to listen to what my body had been telling me for years – I had always considered myself to be strong and fit and now suddenly all my physical strength had left me. No one could explain why nor could they tell me how to get well again – I was fortunate to have the most supportive and helpful GPs, but they had no answers other than to rest with a prognosis of a possible recovery in a few years' time. Well, I didn't want to wait for years – there had to be an answer somewhere, it was just a question of looking in the right place. As it turned out I didn't have to look very far. I had heard of alternative or complementary medicine but had never taken it seriously. In some of the books I had read on M.E., many had been listed as 'tried and failed' by the authors. However I was persuaded by a friend to visit a homeopath and healer and I also consulted a radionics practitioner. After years of chronic illness, unbeknown then to me, I had reached a major turning point. My whole outlook on life was to change as I was introduced to the concepts of holistic medicine and associated therapies. It was these practitioners who first drew my attention to Tai Chi.

Just as there is no single cause of M.E., there is no single road back from it either, but I would say that Tai Chi proved to be a significant factor in my recovery. I had reached a point where I could barely sit upright in a chair, I had no muscle tone or stamina to speak of just to utter a sentence was exhausting. Exercise of any kind seemed out of the question, but as my holistic treatment began to show signs of working, I knew that some form of physical activity was going to have to be considered if I was ever going to get to where I wanted to be. The homeopath had told me it would take about nine months to get me back on my feel and able to cope with the basic demands of life – I got there in eight, and wanted to be able to do more. All that I knew about Tai Chi at this point was that it was of Eastern origin, and I had a picture in my mind of solitary figures standing motionless in beautiful parklands for hours at a time. I had no idea at all of what was involved and was still very fearful of doing anything that might cause me to relapse. However those responsible for my healing to date persuaded me that it was a good idea and when I saw Mark's new class advertised, I enrolled.

It was an effort at first. The class took place in a large school at the top of a flight of stairs which I viewed with some trepidation. However, I was able to rest when I go to the top and I found that there was no pressure on me during the class to do anything which I considered to be too taxing. If I wanted to simply sit out and watch, it was not a problem, although in actual fact by the time I had gone through the warm-up exercises, I rarely found the need to do so. I quickly discovered that the benefits to my circulation were considerable and far from leaving a session fatigued, I always experienced an increased level of energy as well as a general sense of relaxation and well being.

My sleep pattern improved as did my stamina and I quickly realised the benefits of practicing for at least a few minutes every day. Soon I felt able to do other forms of exercise, but I have continued with my Tai Chi and recognise its importance in my daily routine as a factor in preserving my now good health. In the mornings it kick-starts my system wonderfully well. It helps to get the energy flowing, unblocking the channels which get clogged up through the demands we place upon ourselves in modern living, and helps to restore the body's natural balance. To anyone who is attempting to recover from M.E., I cannot recommend the practice of Tai Chi highly enough as a means of breaking in the endless circle of 'I'm-too-ill-to-exercise-therefore-I-shall-become-increasingly-unfit-and-even-more-sick!'
Even if all you can do to start with is sit in a chair and do the breathing exercises, the effects are surprisingly beneficial, and it is a starting point. It is a very gentle but effective way to exercise, placing no real stress on the body or minds and can be done in the quiet of your own home to whatever level you feel you are able to attain. I can now ride, swim, jog and do a day's work with no ill effects and believe that I am probably fitter than a lot of other people.

A holistic approach to treating my condition has been the focal point of my recovery and Tai Chi has been an integral part of that. I believe that it could prove to be of considerable value to people like me in their quest to improve and maintain their health. Wherever they are, I wish them well!

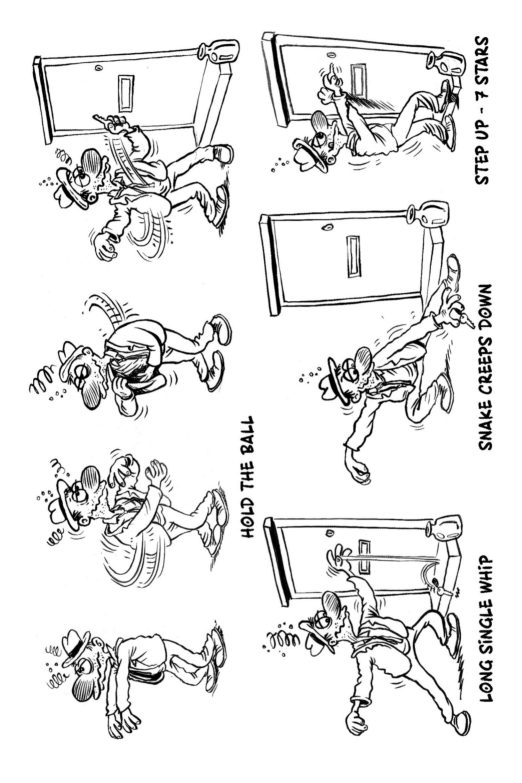

PAT THE TIGER

SPiN

EMBRACE TIGER RETURN TO MOUNTAIN

Live Your Life with the Least Resistance

Punch a head

Punch a wall

Force meets force – the result – pain …

External meets external

Punch the air

Punch a sheet of silk

Force meets nothing – the result – force is confused

External meets internal

LOW PUNCH

34

Tai Chi – A Kiss 'n' Tell Exposé

It was 1990 when the relationship began. When I first heard about Tai Chi, I thought what an interesting sounding name he had. I knew then that if I should ever become involved with him, it would quickly become serious and change my whole life; little did I realise how profoundly.

However, back to the beginning. I had heard his name many times over the years. Friends and acquaintances sometimes spoke of him with awe and said how hard he could be to understand. He sounded a very complicated, mystical person, but if you really got to know him you would see what a good heart he had. Some spoke with great appreciation for the understanding and peace he had brought to their lives. At the time I thought he sounded a little feminine, but they said this was an aspect of his make up and served to balance him, enabling him to encompass all people.

Then a few years ago I started noticing his name in night school brochures, and he always seemed to be in the crowd when the TV ran footage of the Far East. He seemed to be everywhere, on books and magazines; I just couldn't avoid him. I decided to find out more and went to the library to begin my search. The only book available that day was by Danny Connor. I got home, sat in a chair on the patio and started to read. I finished after 3 hours and had to reluctantly put the book down. I felt this was whom I had been looking for for a long time. Someone who could help me relax, grow as an individual, improve my health, and as a bonus, teach me to defend myself.

So in January 1990 I took my first steps of my involvement with *Tai Chi Chuan*. I knew it was going to be hard to get close to him, because many also needed him in their lives. People can be very impatient, if you aren't really committed and willing to accept the knockbacks he can give you, there will be times when you just feel you'll never attain the qualities and skills that he demands if your relationship is going to last.

I saw him every week sometimes twice or three times. He is a hard taskmaster; just reading about him, watching videos and listening to him is not enough, you have to want to be him. In your heart you have to believe that all of his qualities and strengths can be yours. It was hard to get close enough to his essence to understand how he could have so many different qualities. He was a conflict of experiences: powerful but gentle, internal but at the same time powerfully explosive, frustrating but fulfilling, complex but at times suddenly clear. Over the years I have realised that he has changed my life dramatically. It has been hard at times to stay committed and to accept that I was progressing as a person. The more I understood him and his intricacies the more I enjoyed my life; the people I met because of him became a kind of extended family. Plus surprise, surprise I can now defend myself in the way *Tai Chi* promised, because due to his honesty he shares with us family secrets that go back centuries.

Like all relationships there are times when we don't get on and I feel the need to have a break. But when we get together I realise how much I've missed him and it is only the pressures I put on myself that need to be looked at.

There are many impostors who try to emulate his gifts and skills, taking his name without knowing its real meaning. Thank goodness I found *the real Tai Chi*, I could have so easily been misled. If you want to find him, he's tried to make it easier for you by forming the Tai Chi Union for Great Britain and registering with the British Council for Martial Arts in an attempt to keep the usurpers at bay. You just need to make sure that the Tai Chi you seek out can offer you all the things that are important in this life – health, mental and physical security, and plenty of fun. Hopefully your relationship with him will be as long and fruitful as mine. *He is the ultimate peaceful warrior.*

HEEL KICK

SNAKE CREEPS DOWN

35

Not Forgetting the Women

"My painful knees have improved so much."

"The mobility in my aching neck is unbelievably better."

"I realised that I wasn't using my inhaler as much."

"My stomach problems seem to have subsided."

"I can cope with the stress in my life now."

These remarks all came from people who do Tai Chi. The origins of the expression "the thinking man's martial art" may be the same as that Tai Chi has an inherent softness of movement. It is said that the art originated among the ranks of monks and scholars, rather than from fighting men and warriors. Be that as it may, it uses an energy which is very different from that of the fighting man. The monks and scholars possibly wanted to defend themselves in a less violent way, and so searched for such a method, eventually producing the idea of moving more from inside, from the internal energy, and so not damaging one's own body in the process.

Patience

Such men appreciated the importance of patience. Patience is not in plentiful supply in our society, and the old saying that if something is worth having it is worth waiting for goes unobserved. When I had been studying Tai Chi for five years I looked back and realised that I had come a long way, relatively speaking, both martial and health wise. My life seemed broader somehow, and my general awareness improved. Students of the art usually are quite social, in my experience, and if they are not, at the outset, they soon become so. I feel this is because they are looking for more than an hour of instruction. Those who stay after the first few months seem to find that the art becomes an integral part of everyday life. They train the body in the physical and the mind in the mental aspects and slowly the two come together.

You need to feel Tai Chi, and this is what comes to the dedicated student. At times I have become something of an evangelist when extolling the virtues of the art. As a general rule, women are in a minority in the world of martial arts. In my view it is better for women to learn a 'soft' or internal martial art such as Tai Chi, because it is a fact that men are basically much stronger than women and when it comes to the crunch in real combat they are likely to come off worse. Even if a woman learns a tough external art, her body is not as a rule capable of withstanding a hard onslaught from a man. Women are fundamentally softer than men and can, in Tai Chi, take advantage of this fact, since in a sense the art lends itself to that quality.

Balance

In my view, we can use the softness, in Push Hands for example, to draw men in and cause them to lose their balance. Cheng Man-ch'ing himself said that women are more naturally gifted in Tai Chi, so we should use this to help ourselves in confronting men. Not to oppose force with force but with a degree of yielding softness. It usually takes men much longer than women to learn this aspect, the yielding, but of course it has to be learned and incorporated by women also when it comes to the Push Hands of the art.

Appling the virtues of softness is frustrating and difficult and all sincere push hands students, men and women, must confront this problem. Recently during a push hands session we changed partners and I found myself facing a "young buck" who had recently come from hard external martial arts to Tai Chi. During that session he had been pushing with only male students. As we began to 'play' and he had to invest in loss, he suddenly exclaimed, "Just what I need, I'm actually using my waist again instead of having to pile straight through with brute force." Obviously I thrashed him regardless, but who am I to show off …

Investing in loss

It becomes clear that to reap the benefits of health from Tai Chi, relaxation and softness are essential and this is the great gift which we women can bring to the class. Over my years of training in push hands, many times women students have complained to me that they dislike pushing with men because the man's ego sometimes gets in the way. Though it is hard for a man to learn investing in loss, for women it is sometimes, paradoxically harder, because in spite of having an inherent softness, as soon as a woman gains some advantage, then a male partner comes out with brute force, because he is losing his balance. A more experienced woman knows that as a man increases in hardness, ego threatened, the easier it becomes to unbalance him further. But the less experienced woman does not know this, feels threatened, and begins to resort to force, herself.

For this reason, at Kai Ming, we do not introduce push hands until a student has had at least three months of regular training. Students need to know one another and their teacher, for confidence to build. During this period the students begin to know their own space, feel at ease, and this enables them to meet push hands in a much more favourable atmosphere when they begin it.

It must be difficult for the external martial artist to understand why the Tai Chi Chuan student sees his art as a serious self defence method. It is not unknown for us to be the butt of the odd joke or two as the slow, graceful movements are observed. But as the years go by and external martial arts produce muscle strain, broken bones and tension, the Tai Chi student continues to be able to move with ease, with almost no injury results present in the body. Perhaps a case of the tortoise beating the hare.

Practical problems

We sometimes forget that as our fellow students progress there is no realistic prospect of emulating a true to life fighting situation to test their abilities in that direction. So how do we solve this problem? I personally practise any new technique on my son who is six feet four inches tall. Due to my success in eluding his grabs, throttlings and lunges and his frequent requests for cold compresses we both have to accept that the methods do work.

It is a sad fact that in this day and age we cannot escape the reality of violence in our society. An unprovoked attack is particularly important to women. I strongly suggest that Tai Chi is a very good first step in protecting oneself from such attacks. As a registered nurse I can say that a large percentage, perhaps fifty per cent, of problems I see in patients are either caused by stress or are stress related. To some extent, external martial arts increase stress, both physical and mental, accelerating the adrenalin output with all its consequences. I realise that some people enjoy the tough training methods, and find that 'hard' sessions release their stress and aggressions. But I feel these people are the exception rather than the rule. Ultimately their joints will remind them in later life of their earlier training days.

When asked the question, "Why learn Tai Chi?", Cheng Man-ch'ing replied, "When you get to that point in your life when you know what you want, Tai Chi will provide you with the strength to enjoy it." How can we argue with that?

Mark Peters with
Master Tan Ching Nee

36

Masters Like Chocolate Too

I'm looking through the kitchen window which overlooks our patio. Out in the cold morning air, heralding the onset of winter, my husband Mark Peters is learning the spear form, as he has been 'instructed' to do by his Sifu, Master Tan Ching Ngee of Singapore. The birds seem to be watching with interest from the safety of tall trees scattered around the garden; they are silent.

Sweat rolls down his forehead, despite the chill; Chi seems to defy the elements. Then Master Tan appears at the patio doors, watching intensely, sometimes nodding with approval, and then tapping the window to convey corrections. Then, unable it seems to resist his inclinations, he slips on a pair of gloves against the unfamiliar English cold and steps out to join his student. Frost glints in the early morning sun as they begin to train together.

The student is eager to learn and carry on traditions, and the Master perhaps re-lives his own training days with Grandmaster Cheng Man-ch'ing; days when he, like Mark, could never quench his thirst for the secrets which Tai Chi holds. They move together, sometimes serious and sometimes laughing out loud when Mark makes a silly mistake. I must be getting sentimental, because for a second I am so touched that I feel a surge of emotion and tears well up. Moments such as these are too few. In a back garden in Birmingham, East meets West as student and teacher unite in a love for the art that nourishes them both.

Just as I turn away, I hear a voice which usually speaks very little English vibrate across the patio, "You must train very hard, I no teach crap Kung fu." Perhaps Singapore is not so far away after all.

Arrival

As we waited in the busy arrival hall at Heathrow airport for the passengers from Kuala Lumpur, we wondered what lay ahead during the week to come. We were waiting to meet a Tai Chi Master who is one of the dwindling number of disciples of Grandmaster Cheng Man-ch'ing, the diminutive man who could fill a room with the power of his form, and the founder of the style of Tai Chi which we practise.

Our club, Kai Ming, had invited Master Tan Ching Ngee to visit England and pass on some of his vast knowledge of the martial arts, by holding seminars in Scotland and Birmingham. This was January 1997, and at last in October, all the arrangements had borne fruit. Master Tan is a doctor and his clinic in Singapore made it impossible for him to give us more than a week of his time. Everyone was determined to make as much of this one week as possible.

Second visit

The seminars were fully booked. We had not seen him for four years, and on that occasion his visit had been blemished by the behaviour of a man of no honour, culminating in much bad feeling. We are no longer associated with that individual.

We did not know what to expect when Master Tan arrived, and wondered if this visit would be coloured by the events of his previous visit and cause him to hold back from passing on his knowledge to us. Suddenly we caught sight of a familiar face. He is not a powerfully built man but gives off an undoubted presence. As we began our journey back to Birmingham the conversation was limited; he speaks little English and we do not speak Chinese. But as time passed I believed I could sense a certain distance from us, as if he were wondering if his reception would be the same as before.

Seminar

The weekend seminar was a huge success. Even though all his teaching was through an interpreter (many thanks to Terry and Fay Yip), nothing was lost and we hung on his every word. There were numerous questions, and Master Tan worked tirelessly with depth and frankness. He told us that it was the small points, the details, which made the difference and he made sure that we understood these. Two days passed, and everyone went home somewhat exhausted but very happy in the knowledge that their understanding of Tai Chi had improved. I know that I speak for all of us when I say that we felt we had been with a great Master.

As the week moved on it seemed Master Tan was growing more at ease, and it was obvious that he enjoyed being with so many keen Western students. Both his skill and his speed impressed everyone. Where many of us only dream of training with a disciple of Grandmaster Cheng, here we were actually with one of them. All who met him fell under his spell. So as he warmed to us he began to try to communicate in broken English which far outstripped our Chinese.

In between teaching, we took him on a quest for Chinese antiques and as luck would have it the 'Big Brum' antiques fair took place during his visit, starting at 6.30 a.m.! There were one thousand two hundred stalls and I am sure that Master Tan saw them all. His knowledge was impressive and much heated bargaining went on that day. Here was someone who could tell the dealers a few things, no mistake.

I warmed to Master Tan as the days passed, and we shared many a joke. The Cadbury World visit showed us that even Tai Chi Masters like chocolate and there were, when he returned to Singapore, quite a few bars of it in his fridge.

Dignity

Throughout his visit, whether teaching, reminiscing about his days with Cheng Man-ch'ing, or laughing uproariously when Mark dropped the supermarket bag and smashed his beer bottles, there was an air of dignity about him. There was the feeling that this Master not only taught 'Good Kung fu' but if necessary would be able to use it very effectively.

There are many self-proclaimed 'Masters' around the world but I learned that week that it takes much more than a martial skill to command respect and loyalty. A good heart is needed in a teacher, and if this not present you will learn precious little. The teacher will keep things to himself or herself, afraid to pass on too much in case one day you are equal to him, equal to her. Such a teacher will treat you badly and bask in his own glory, self centred at the expense of the pupils. But a good heart radiates from Master Tan and those who treated him badly did him a great injustice.

As his plane soared upwards, bound for Singapore, I hoped that he took back with him a very different impression of British students and martial artists. I remembered his inscription on a fan which he gave me: "Money cannot buy you a good heart, but Tai Chi can." Zai Jian Master Tan may we meet again soon.

A NOTE OF CLARIFICATION

Master Tan's approach to the art was that slow movement can be to slow and develop listening skills (ting jing) to decide the appropriate speed of both practice and application. He said Master Cheng often practiced his 37 step form at a quicker pace to develop free-flowing movement and balance. The ability to flow from quick to slow is not restricted to Chen style alone and should apply to all styles. Following-step training helps with moving push-hands to enhance the flow.

Master Cheng has been quoted as saying that all the skill (Gong Fu) is in the transition from one movement/posture to another and Master Tan said this meant that it is easy to stand still but great skilfulness and personal awareness are required to move with balance and awareness from one form posture to the next; to maintain the natural ebb and flow or swing and return (Dong Dang). To move from form to natural push-hands requires a keen sense of this ebb and flow to enable us to naturally find the openings and apply the art freely.

To practice tai chi without any understanding of its application makes no sense at all. Both its application in fighting and its application for life are essential. Too many people just say that they practice tai chi but practice is not enough to gain any real benefits, you have to live it in all aspects of your life.

Master Tan says that tai chi is a natural art and as such flows and evolves as does a river; it should not stagnate like a still pond. If Master Cheng had rigidly stuck to Yang Cheng Fu's teachings he would have failed his teacher and the art. We should all strive to continue the development of tai chi chuan whilst maintaining its core principle. We should all look to the classics for help with this.

We hope having read the chapters of this book, you are inspired to continue or even begin your Tai Chi journey. If along the way you feel you have a story to tell and share, please send it to us at Kai Ming.

markpeters@kaiming.co.uk

Visit www.kaiming.co.uk for more contact details.